The Tao of Spiritual Partnership

Background Music in Daily Life That Can
Enhance Your Growth

Gabriella Kortsch, Ph.D.

Advance Praise for

The Tao of Spiritual Partnership

"All humans seek the illusive touch of another's Soul, which opens us to the sense of belonging to something bigger than the self. Dr. Kortsch has given us the true "tao" of relationship in this brilliant exploration of emotional tapestry. Through her wise teaching, we can not only discover ourselves in the reflection of our partners, but we can learn how to access a *spiritual* connection that sets us free. We will be grateful for this illumination of spiritual partnership for generations to come. Thank You, Gabriella."

Chris Griscom: Spiritual Leader, Author

"In my years of researching life plans and soul contracts, I've learned that we plan (before we're born) to have romantic relationships for the purposes of healing and expansion. And this is just what Gabriella Kortsch so eloquently and comprehensively shows you in *The Tao of Spiritual Partnership*: how your primary love relationship may be a sacred vessel that transports you and your partner to a place of mutual healing and expansion."

Robert Schwartz: Author of *Your Soul's Gift: The Healing Power of the Life You Planned Before You Were Born*

"Riveting introduction into the author's life, authentically reflecting her years of personal development and truths. I cried, I reflected, and then I merged my soul with the truthfulness of the facts as presented. Gabriella Kortsch takes us through a journey that covers most aspects of human relationships from new-born to adult, leading us into the power and path of Spiritual Partnerships and what it all means, what to do with it, and how to apply it to our lives, in this precise moment in time. The importance of fulfillment of a life well-lived through understanding and practicing self-love is paramount and candidly expressed in this one-of-a-kind book. I have gained deeper insights into my own life, and the promise of the book: "to love without needing" is profoundly delivered!

Ali R. Rodriguez: Business Coach Strategist, Co-Author of *Mastering the Art of Success* with Les Brown and Jack Canfield

"The *Tao of Spiritual Partnership* is an excellent, smart guide to making your relationships blossom. Your partner will thank you for buying this book! Why struggle with relationships when you can have a fulfilling spiritual partnership? Dr. Gabriella Kortsch's newest book ·The *Tao of Spiritual Partnership* deftly shows the way to satisfying interactions with the loves of your life."

Jim Wawro, Author of *Awakening Counsel: A Practical Guide to Creating the Life You Want to Live.*

"Gabriella Kortsch has a rich international background with unmatched experience in her field. The *Tao of Spiritual Partnership* is a unique blend of wit and wisdom; she encourages us to take responsibility for our relationships, while recognizing and seizing the opportunities for our own personal spiritual growth."

William Buhlman, Author of *Adventures Beyond the Body*

Also by Gabriella Kortsch, Ph.D.

BOOKS

Rewiring the Soul: Finding the Possible Self

WORKSHOP CD's

(available on the website)

**Relationships: Priceless Tools for Self-Understanding,
Growth, and Inner Freedom**
(4-Hour Audio CD Workshop)

**Fatherless Women and Motherless Men: The Influence
of Absent Parents on Adult Relationships**
(4-Hour Audio CD Workshop)

The Tao of Spiritual Partnership

Background Music in Daily Life That Can Enhance Your Growth

Gabriella Kortsch, Ph.D.

Cover Design by Ignacio Martel

Library of Congress Cataloging-in-Publication Data

Kortsch, Gabriella

The tao of spiritual partnership: background music in daily life that can enhance your growth / Gabriella Kortsch.

Includes biographical references and index.

ISBN-13: 978 – 1479180189

ISBN-10: 1479180181

1. Spiritual life 2. Love 3. Happiness 3. Relationships 4. Wisdom 5. Mental Healing I. Kortsch, Gabriella II. Title

2012916279

Dedicated to all those I love and have loved and who have loved me; to those that I carry in my heart, and who have carried me in yours, although you may no longer be here. You have shown me the infinite variety of faces that give such rich meaning to love.

CONTENTS

Introduction:

The False Hope of Conventional Relationships

Spiritual partnership - more exciting than any other kind of relationship you have ever known - is a path - *a Tao* - offered to us to evolve and grow. It is my deep wish that as you read this book and apply its principles to your life, you will find momentum, encouragement, and inspiration to pave your way to a different and new kind of partnership. In so doing, it is also my deep wish that you will find that connection to yourself that will allow you to live in the greatest inner peace, harmony and well-being you have ever experienced. Spiritual partnership is a path we can choose to take in order to make this possible. Spiritual partnership acts as background music in your daily life allowing you - should you so decide - to enhance your process of evolution and growth. Loving another individual - a life partner, a parent, a child, a friend - brings this possibility into our lives, initially through pain and frustration because, as you will come to recognize as you read, how we are led to understand love and relationship in our culture has little to do with true spiritual partnership where love lies in an entirely different dimension.

It is *precisely* at the problematic crossroads so often encountered in relationships that we are offered the opportunity to create a new foundation based on mutual complementarity rather than need; a free relationship between two people who *want* to be together, rather than two people who *need* to be together. Needing another, we are told, is the measure of love, but for a fully conscious individual *nothing could be further from the truth*. And therein lies part of the secret and healing power of spiritual partnerships.

****

When I was five my family moved from Germany to Canada. One day as I played in the home of friends of my parents - very elderly friends - I caught myself listening with bated breath to a conversation taking place among the adults in the next room. Our hostess was telling the others about her sister who had died. But then, so she related, a being surrounded by light had come to save her. The lady called that being an angel. And now her sister was alive again. I was riveted to my chair as I heard this - and to this day, over five decades later, I can vividly remember the feeling - and then, as the story continued, I recognized that what was being said was something that felt familiar, almost as though I had already known about beings of light that saved people from dying. And the story continued as I carried on eavesdropping: the lady who had died had entered a dark tunnel. At the end of the dark tunnel she had met the 'angel'. And he had told her that she had to go back and remain on earth. While I really had no idea who or what this being of light was, I *knew* there was something or someone waiting at the end of that tunnel and this *knowing* was familiar, and I also *knew* about the tunnel, but exactly *who* the someone at the end was, remained elusive to me. I also knew that knowing all of this was very important, although at that stage I had no idea why.

At fifteen, visiting my father in Switzerland one summer, he was in the midst of a relationship with an enigmatic, mysterious, and highly charismatic woman. I admired much about her and wished to emulate her multi-faceted base of knowledge.

Conversations sparked with eclectic rarity and electrical charges when she was present, and I always looked forward to our interaction. There was also much intrigue about her and her mesmerizingly international background. On a road trip to Rome through the verdant Italian countryside, I observed her and my father interacting with much tumultuousness and wondered - with not a small amount of aversion in my teenage heart and brain - how they could know so much about such a multitude of fascinating subjects, and yet - on a relationship basis - know so little.

A year or two later, well into all manner of teenage experimentation, I visited my brother in Montreal. Our common religious upbringing in a highly fundamentalist vein, which both of us had roundly rejected, nevertheless allowed us to understand each other when issues arose. In this case I wondered if I had sinned, and hence, if that meant that I was no longer 'good'. He was nine years older and from the height - for me at that time - of his superior knowledge, he looked at me tenderly with all the love his heart held for me and that encompassed me with warm and gentle kindness as he spoke, and assured me that I was indeed *good*. My feeling of relief was palpable and my thoughts about him centered on the puzzle of how he had become so non-judgmental. Where had he learned how to be like this? None of the other members of both my immediate and extended family appeared to be like that at all, religious fervor notwithstanding.

My mother died unexpectedly around my 20th birthday and three years later I stood over the casket of my loving and non-judgmental brother as well, cradling a newborn baby in my arms, my strong and beautiful eldest son. Both my mother and brother had died of cancer and something in me seemed to have died as well. Less than two years later my second son was born, and eventually I began to feel alive again. My third son, who arrived another 16 months after that, nearly ripped me out of my foundations as we found him floating at the bottom of the pool when he was less than a year old. We were blessed that afternoon in a Houston suburb, and with the help of our then Uruguayan housekeeper Elena, we managed to resuscitate him and eventually our pediatrician and the neurologist proclaimed him to be in perfect health despite the approximate five minutes we calculated he had been under water. Why, I asked myself, do these things happen? What did it mean? I continually feared he would die, and indeed, he suffered all manner of strange accidents and miraculous recoveries. He was still quite a little boy when I finally learned, thanks to a shaman I met in a bookstore in a very bourgeois Swiss neighbourhood, to let go of my fear of his death. Interestingly, he never had any further strange accidents.

The next years of my life proved to be so difficult, heart-breaking, and painful that I often believed I would not survive. Much of this had to do with an excessively negative outcome to a failed marriage. This caused me to spend a good deal of time - not only in those years, but also in later years - in thought and study about relationships and the blindness of individuals' reactions (my own included) to each other.

Several years later at the beginning of 1990 I moved from southern Spain to Mexico, to the Yucatan Peninsula where I immersed myself in the lure and mystery of Mayan archaeology. I was to remain there for nearly six years. I told friends of my yearning for a newsletter that would keep me informed of the entire gamut of the latest advances in all fields. I remarked having read that John F. Kennedy had surrounded himself with advisors who kept him abreast of the newest developments in all disciplines, and that for me, this must have been one of the most magnificent perks of being the president of the United States. Barely a year later the internet became a reality in my life. Not, I hasten to add, the internet as we know it today, with search engines that appear almost magical in their speed of offering us data about any type of knowledge, no matter how obscure, but nevertheless, an internet that connected anyone with a computer to vast arenas of information. It was so exciting to be alive!

At this time I was also becoming aware of the latest in mind-body research, known as psycho-neuro-immunology or PNI, and I clearly remember sitting at an elegant dinner party in Mexico City, creating quite a few politely raised eyebrows as I spoke of the connection between stress or bitterness, pain, disillusion, and resentment and an ultimate outcome such as cancer.

Brain research was beginning to inform the world of its findings: our brains do not have to go into decline, but can continue growing as long as we are alive, with the caveat that we cannot stop learning; connections between brain cells and actual neurons themselves go on multiplying, and the term neuro-plasticity, referring to the flexibility of the brain at all ages began to appear. Quantum physics told us of sub-atomic particles, of quarks and strings, but it also began talking of something that sounded suspiciously like metaphysics when it said that at some level the entire universe is connected energetically, and that therefore in some way *we are all one*.

And still around this time, such a rich period of learning in my life, in 1991, I visited the Light Institute in Galisteo, New Mexico for the second time to undergo regression therapy. Connecting to some of my past lives taught me about forgiving and the magic that such forgiving can effect in relationships, and that *knowing* changed so much in my life. It is perhaps, one of the greatest lessons I have learned. It also helped me connect so many of the threads in my life in order to come to greater understanding of how we as individuals can grow exponentially thanks to our relationships. (For a more detailed account of my experiences at the Light Institute, see *Rewiring the Soul*).

From Mexico I returned to the USA, this time to Miami where as I approached mid-life I decided to embark on a doctoral degree in psychology. Again, as in other chapters of my life, I was consumed with much contemplation, study and writing about the subject of relationships and how our early connections affect our adult emotional life to such a large degree.

Some years later, after returning to Spain, on the eve of Valentine's Day in 2006 I received an innocuous looking fax at my office. It stated rather baldly that I had a malignant carcinoma - uterine cancer. Since both my mother and brother had themselves died very early of cancer, the latter at age 31 of a very malignant and virulent form of melanoma, and the former at the age of 54 of what doctors termed a 'galloping' uterine cancer - a very similar kind to the one I had just been diagnosed with - it occurred to me that perhaps the members of my very small family were doomed. WW II had decimated some parts of the family, leaving siblings and parents of some of my relatives missing in parts unknown, with no knowledge of where and how they might have died, and although this occurred before my own birth, these stories formed an intrinsic and poignant part of my childhood. My mother's own flight from Prussia to Western Germany as the Russians advanced into what we now know as Poland, bearing only her small baby - my brother - some diapers for him and all the negatives of the photographs she did not want to lose, had always formed a large part of my childhood imagination about something I could barely fathom.

Failed relationships tinged with deep pain and the endless regret of what had not been able to be, marked us all. Enormous geographical separations from those we most loved further left their indelible print, necessitating frequent heart-wrenching good-byes in cold, antiseptic train stations and airports. A part of me almost didn't care about the cancer.

But I had learned so much over the years: personally, emotionally, and professionally. I *knew* that whatever the final outcome of the cancer, my life in the meantime could be *good.* And so I began a systematic re-organization of my inner and outer well-being, looking at all those things that I already knew, but that I had not applied totally to my life in a conscious and conscientious way. My first book *Rewiring the Soul* as a path to inner and outer growth was born out of that process. I healed myself - and I refer to my total self, not just the part of me that had cancer - by standing at what Frans Johansson calls the *intersection* in his book *The Medici Effect*: the intersection of all these diverse and even unrelated things that had interested and affected me over the years of my life, that I had learned from not only in the class room and lecture hall or by reading, but also by observing and applying, living and suffering, and eventually - at the moment of my diagnosis - by bringing it together synergistically to create a healthier self.

This all is closely connected to spiritual partnership. But first, let's have a look at love. What does love offer us?

Getting Our Needs Fulfilled

I need to warn you: I'm making a great distinction between falling in love and loving. The difference is not generally understood. Often people either believe that the two are the same or that the latter – loving – is less exciting than being in love, somehow equating loving to the emotions you feel for your parents or children or good friends or pets; emotions that can be very strong, but that tend to be much less exhilarating than the other.

In the former case you fall in love with that which fills your needs. You love someone because you receive something you need from them. Not necessarily something material, as much as an inner need they are fulfilling for you because you have not yet learned how to fulfill it for yourself. You may not even be aware of the fact that it (fulfilling your own needs) is something you should be doing. And as long as that is so, you will depend on the other person remaining the way they are just at the moment you fall in love, in order to feel good. Your well-being will depend, to a large degree, on that factor, which means, of course, that you will never be independent.

Dependence and Independence

The topic of dependence and independence particularly in love relationships, but also in others, is of vast importance. Think of the fact that due to your need of the other, and hence your desire to continue feeling as good as you feel when you are with that person, as well as your desire that he/she continues to behave in the way that makes you feel so good, you may do some of the following in order to maintain that particular status quo:

- You may neglect your other interests, if these interests are not of importance to your partner. In some fashion, therefore, we might say that you are neglecting your own life. And this is very important because when you may need the *support* of those interests in your life at some future point, you will be disconnected from them. (Interests can support you because when things are difficult in other areas of your life, they can help hold you up, *precisely* because they capture your attention in critical ways and hence are capable of giving meaning to your life, something which is *always* of significance, but tremendously important during bad times).
- You may neglect your friends in order to spend more time with your partner. This is crucial because when you may need that social network at some future point it, the network - your friends - may no longer be available to you.

- You may decide to give up certain ideas and opinions in order to mold yourself more closely to your partner. If you think only a wimp would do this, only someone with no character and no moral fiber, allow me to remind you of the fact that we are extremely good at rationalizing and convincing ourselves that we are doing something because *we really want to* and only recognize after the facts that we did indeed drop those ideas and opinions to fit in better, or to please the other. And lest it be thought that I am advocating never pleasing the other that is most definitely not the case. But it *is* a case of being very conscious and clear about what is going on when you do so. You might please the other with an article of clothing, a certain type of perfume, taking up a sport (if you really want to and really enjoy it), or any other example you care to mention, but if you convert to Judaism or Catholicism or Buddhism mainly to please the other, or if you change political parties to please the other (or to have a better atmosphere at home), or if you start (or stop) smoking to please the other, or start going to the opera or football games to please the other, then do make absolutely certain that you are, in fact, also pleasing yourself.
- You may ultimately *lose* a portion of yourself by doing some of the above or similar things because in some ways that are not healthy, you will have become fused with the other person, and this *lost* portion of yourself will only then come back into your consciousness when you either recognize what has happened, or perhaps when the relationship breaks up. Losing this part of yourself to please another or to have a relationship without problems, or because you want to continue feeling the way you did at the beginning, is a very large price to pay.

A Healthy Dose of Self-Love

However, in the other case – the case where your love is independent of need - you love someone but you do not need them because you have taken care of yourself (or begun the process of taking care of yourself) with a healthy dose of self-love. You simply love without expectation. Rather a tall order. Much of beauty has been written about this latter kind of love.

In this case, because you do not need, because you love without expectation, you will never - or no longer - be dependent, and you will always be free. And this doesn't mean, by the way, that you accept anything just because you have no expectations. On the contrary, because you are free of boundary issues, self esteem issues, and neediness issues, you find it very easy to speak up in healthy ways about anything that you *do* find unacceptable.

Is the 'Love' You Experience When You 'Fall in Love' Inferior ?

So if loving is so good, and the way I am making it sound, falling in love is something of a far inferior quality, then is there a good thing about falling in love? Yes! In fact, there is a very wonderful thing about falling in love.

It's this: it takes you - if you allow it - down the road towards the other kind of love. The *falling in love* kind of love, takes you to a place of learning and growth because of the deep frustration and pain it generally brings along with it - at least after a while.

So falling in love often leads to frustration and pain and that leads you to growth. And growth, in turn, leads you - eventually - not only to inner freedom, but particularly, to the recognition that as long as you need another, as long as you depend on another to fulfill your needs, you will never love in the true sense of the word. You begin to recognize that fulfilling your own needs is part of true adult self-responsibility, self-love and maturity, as is – even more importantly – taking on the responsibility for your own well-being, as opposed to leaving it in the hands of your partner.

I Love You Because I Need You

Why do we believe we love because we need? Is there any part of that kind of sentiment that is mature and adult? Where else can it lead us other than to - eventual - frustration and pain? And don't forget: if the other person is also on the same page and loves you because of how you fill *their* needs, then they will go through a similar process. And sooner or later you are going to let them down – as they will let you down – because it is very difficult to be *responsible for another's well-being by fulfilling their needs*, the needs that they should be fulfilling themselves.

So to fall in love and go through this process is excellent because the place we come out at the other end of the tunnel is indeed worth its weight in gold. To love without needing is the priceless gift we can receive from having fallen in love and having chosen to use the challenges it evokes to further our growth, rather than to take the simple way out and blame the other for now no longer fulfilling our needs, or no longer making us happy. Having fallen in love is the basic step that can lead us to the treasure of being able to love without needing.

But let's take a step back. We haven't yet discovered how loving without needing can be possible. To arrive at such a prospect is the promise of this book.

In order to lay the foundation for that, let's first examine the state of marriages and relationships in our 21st century. Who isn't familiar with the continually escalating statistics about marriages going sour? They seem to last less and less time, and families appear destined to suffer the trauma and pain of break ups and divorce. Obviously we are concerned about the effect of this on our children, but there is no doubt that the original partners in a relationship bear countless painful consequences as well. And as we see the numbers rise, and watch our friends and family go through the depressingly familiar process of splitting in two, the question whether anything can be done about it makes its clamoring voice heard more and more loudly.

Historically, and particularly in the 1960's, as society moved gradually from a patriarchal paradigm to one that we might call slightly more egalitarian, divorce figures began to creep up as more and more women found themselves enabled to get an education and have careers, or even just "jobs" outside of the home.

Along with patriarchy, organized religion suffered a blow as well, particularly in the western world, as growing numbers of people began rejecting the norms that had once held them safely within the confines of holy matrimony.

In addition, as the women's movement gained momentum, academically, professionally, socio-economically, and last but not least, biologically, and hence, sexually, women were further released from the biological, social, and financial need to remain with only one man with the advent of the pill during approximately the same timeframe. The double standard began declining in power, and with it, women took off on a run, intent on proving to the world that they could live as freely as men.

In the mid- to late 1970's women slowly began earning salaries that made it feasible for them to care for themselves and their children if need be without necessarily requiring the help of a male. (Before you send off indignant emails, please bear in mind that I am merely sketching in the broad outlines of a painting here. Clearly, many women are still not in such a position, because promotions and salaries remain imbalanced on the scale that lies between the genders, but for our purpose here, let us say that for some women it has become possible.)

Mass media played along as well in the two decades spanning the 70's and 80's, by showing us *Sex and the City*, rather than the home-spun down to earth sitcoms of the 50's. In cinema *Kramer vs. Kramer* moved us to tears, light years from familiar, old standards such as Bing Crosby and Grace Kelly in *High Society*. Glossy magazines such as *Cosmopolitan* advised young women how to have orgasms in one night stands rather than how to organize a wedding reception, and books were published by the dozen with the central theme of women free from the constraints of a male-dominated society.

Finally, we were shown on a large scale that among prominent people, whether politicians, or celebrities from the world of cinema, art and high finance, women could marry and re-marry, or not marry at all and have children on their own, with one or several men, or even adopt children without the benefit of marriage.

In a word: the old idea of marriage clearly no longer works, mainly because it no longer fits into the manner in which the world has changed and evolved, but no truly innovative ideas for marriage have emerged, at least, not any that show any real signs of working.

Some have suggested that one of the main reasons relationships, partnerships, and marriages are no longer working, is that although we try to put our new-found ideas into them, in the hopes that with these ideas, relationships will once again work, the minute we actually marry again, we fall back into our old patriarchal patterns in an almost undermining fashion, as though these patterns were inherent to the very institution of marriage. How many couples have not expressed the sentiment that their relationship was fine while they were living together, and only went down the hill when they decided to get married?

This is not a facetious recommendation to not marry, and hope that by just living together all will be well. Far from it. It may be true, however, that the old institution of marriage is invested with some very profound patterns, and that in order to remove these patterns and put others in their place, we have to look to the very foundations of what we believe a marriage to be.

Partnership for the purpose of procreation and survival in which the two parties do not necessarily see themselves as equals is a way of describing the old pattern. Partnership for the purpose of getting love and being happy is another way of describing the old pattern. The great mythologist Joseph Campbell said in his opus *The Hero's Journey* that people think that relationships are about happiness. But they're not. They're about transformation. *"It's through the relationship that the development of each is taking place."*

Gary Zukav suggests that the new pattern be partnership between equals *for the purpose of spiritual growth*. What this really means is that you start realizing that what is important to the well-being of your relationship is exactly the same as what is needed for your own spiritual growth. Each partner holds the pieces that the other is missing. If you are angry, suspicious, or jealous, for example, then these feelings bring up something in your partner that needs to be healed, and it is precisely that which is being mirrored in you. So you begin to see the importance of your partner's interaction with you for your development (and vice versa).

Spiritual growth does not mean going to church or praying (although you can certainly do that, if you wish), nor does it mean that the importance of physical togetherness and contact is minimized. Quite the contrary. It enhances it. Spiritual growth *does* mean, however, that the common denominator of the relationship becomes the idea that both partners are in the relationship to grow (and love, and trust, and enjoy, etc., but with a continuous eye towards growth).

Eckhart Tolle puts it in slightly different terms and speaks of *enlightened* relationships. He says that when a relationship is not working, what was not conscious in each of the partners is being brought out into the light. He essentially means that by virtue of the problems the relationship starts experiencing, the parts of yourself that you have never seen begin to become apparent. At first, most of what you will see is the blame you are heaping on your partner, and not much of yourself actually comes to the surface, but in time, or after several such relationships, it all has a great opportunity to become conscious and therein lies growth.

The authors Nick Duffel and Helena Lovendal, as well as Eva Pierrakos make similar suggestions. They also refer to the somewhat esoteric concept of relationship as teacher, or spiritual path which eventually leads to a process of transformation for both people. This gives the relationship a sense of purpose that differs immeasurably from the patriarchal or organized religion model. Duffel and Lovendal believe that a couple comes apart (with conflict) for a very specific purpose, so that they can build up a strong charge for the alchemical coming together again, physically, psychologically, and on all levels, as the relationship grows.

Can you do this in one day? Of course not. First you have to be willing to even look at a relationship as something more than a way to have another person that will make you happy. Then you would need to have a conversation with your partner to see what he/she feels about some ideas such as those expressed herein. Then you can get to work. You might start by reading some books such as the one in your hands, attending some workshops, seeing a therapist, and most particularly, learning how to become aware, and learning that you always have choices.

What if you are young, have never been married, and dislike what you've seen out there? You see your parents, your friends' parents, and so many other people who are in unhappy marriages or divorced. You may find that the ideas expressed here give you new insights. Marriage isn't just to be happy, have the house, 1.85 kids, and live together happily ever after. There is another purpose that reaches so much further. Clients who tell me they are not in a relationship, have recently come out of one, and are considering a new one, because they have met someone, but worry that perhaps they should hold off until all their 'issues' are resolved, only get encouragement to move towards the new relationship from me. Why? Because being in a relationship is the second quickest way to grow. Being in a *committed* relationship is the quickest way.

If you are in a marriage that is floundering, you might want to consider the ideas pointed out here. Don't forget that your inner life is continually in flux, including the way you think about relationships. People don't mature once, and then remain that way the rest of their lives. Likewise, they do not get married or get into a committed relationship and then maintain it exactly the way it was the day of the wedding or the commitment. Therefore, there is no reason why you can't evolve your ideas of partnership and look in new directions *within* the parameters of your current relationship along with your partner. Imagine getting a new set of stronger contact lenses or glasses. Imagine how they help you see the world more sharply, more clearly. So too, can you get another perspective on the real purpose of your marriage by considering the material in this book. The deep intrinsic satisfaction and happiness that come from psychological, emotional, and spiritual growth have few parallels.

****

So back to what was stated earlier: this all is strongly connected to spiritual partnership because everything that occurs in our lives is so closely intertwined with ramifications on all levels. Having a spiritual partnership; being equipped to have a spiritual partnership, implies being healthy on all those levels that go far beyond the merely physical and practical. And normally in our dysfunctional world of socialization that leads us down such a wide array of dismayingly stray paths, in order to be healthy so that we are indeed able to have a spiritual partnership, we must first understand how to walk that road to health. Without such a framework we find ourselves like those who go to a gym for the first time, in a maze of gleaming machines, that we don't know how to use, and that we often wind up using incorrectly, and hence do not give our bodies the full benefit of their intended purpose.

The intended purpose of the self is not to suffer, but to grow and to experience joy, and it is most particularly through our human relationships, and especially through our love relationships that we are able to evolve. But - just as in the analogy about the machines at the gym - if we don't know how to go about our relationships, if our framework is erected on erroneous concepts or beliefs and particularly on lack of awareness, then not only will we not grow in the way I've indicated, but we will have little chance at ever experiencing the magnificence of true spiritual partnership.

Chapter 1

Patterns: Same Old ... Same Old

Most of us start out our relationship lives by reliving a pattern we've brought in from childhood. This is not our fault. *It just is*. But it *is* our responsibility to become aware of it, as much as we possibly can, although again, at the beginning we are *not*, and that also simply is not our fault. *It just is*.

It's essentially when the patterns start repeating themselves, that it becomes our responsibility to be conscious enough to become aware of them, as opposed to blaming our partner or our bad luck.

But *why* do we often start our relationship lives that way? What happened in our childhood that caused us to fall into a pattern of some kind? Shall we just blame our parents? The answer to that is a rotund *no*. Even if we could prove that our parents were not good parents, there is simply no point in blaming them. *It solves nothing*. Furthermore, by the time many of us realize that we have such a pattern, and that it might be related to some element of our early upbringing and emotional closeness or lack thereof, we are already in our 30's and 40's or more, and often our parents are no longer around. More than casting our eye about in order to find someone to blame, compassion is the word we need to keep on the front burner when we undergo such realizations, because generally speaking our parents clearly became the way they did due to *their own* upbringing. It's so much more important to focus on the fact that now, thanks to having become aware of the pattern, we can actually *do* something about it in our *own* lives.

And by so doing, we can move beyond it, to another kind of relationship that need not consist of the blindness or the compulsions or obsessions that our earlier relationships have consisted of.

So back to our question of why our relationship lives often begin that way: i.e., through our current relationship, we are typically living out a childhood pattern. Imagine a scenario with an emotionally unavailable parent that the child desperately tries to draw into its circle of love. What happens when the child is unable to do so? There are numerous possible outcomes. One potential result is that the child believes it is unlovable. Or perhaps it believes it is not loved due to its own fault, for not doing this or that or the other *correctly*. It may begin to believe that love is not safe because it hurts. Such a child might become hopeless, but it might *also* become a variant of the genus *over-achiever* in order to garner praise, honor, and approval.

This individual craves such reactions from others because that is how he can finally feel good about himself - even if it's only for that one moment of achievement. Then, of course, he has to go out again and achieve the next thing, in order to get the praise again, so that he can feel good about himself. (Note: another, more healthy and self-loving variant of over-achiever would not need the praise because he would be achieving for the joy of the journey, and *not simply the praise and honor at the end of it.*)

Or imagine a parent who continually criticizes the child, never once giving the child the satisfaction of hearing the words *I am so proud of you ... you did such a good job*. The child simply never feels he/she is good enough. Imagine the devastation this creates in the way one begins to love the self, or better said, imagine how nearly impossible it will be for such a child to begin to love itself, or in any way feel good about itself.

Or imagine having a parent who uses the child's love to manipulate the child emotionally: making it feel guilty or bad or inadequate in some way. This again works against the child's best interests and precludes a healthy love for the self, a strong belief in the self and the necessary acceptance of the self in order to lead a productive life.

Or imagine the parent who shows the child that someone *or something* else (the other parent, a new partner, another sibling, a profession or any kind of an activity, perhaps a sport, or even shopping, a spiritual ideal, or a 'mission') is always more important in the parent's life than the child itself. It makes sense that the adult this child eventually becomes will either be abandoned by the partner, or will be the one who does the abandoning.

Or imagine the parent who in some fashion abandons the child, whether emotionally, physically, financially or in other ways. This not only leaves scars, but also sets the child up for relationships that somehow re-enact some of these abandonment scenarios.

And *that*, in a nutshell, is precisely the reason why we have patterns: on subconscious levels we choose partners with whom we are able to re-enact our unresolved childhood scenarios. Why, you ask, would we want to do this? I don't believe we *want* to do it - at least not consciously - but our psyche somehow knows that it is a process that can lead to healing whatever was wounded in childhood, although of course what heals us is *not* the repetition of a pattern, but the *recognition* of the pattern and the cleansing of the part of the self that got us there - as adults - in the first place. And that recognition, as said, does not generally happen until we have gone through the pain and frustration of a failing or failed relationship, as well as - most of the time - not just one, but several such relationships.

So we subconsciously pick partners that will do for us what our parents did, or what the parent with whom we had the difficulty did. Obviously this does not happen during the honeymoon phase of the relationship, or we would *never* get into the relationship in the first place. We generally first 'cement' our relationships with a marriage certificate, or the joint purchase of a home, or a baby, before we get into the painful part. Some authors believe this cementing occurs (again subconsciously) so that we are unable to easily get out of the relationship and therefore we at least have a chance of trying to understand what is happening, although unfortunately for many of us, that does not always happen, and most particularly, it does not always happen the first time around.

And just to reiterate, *please* do not make the mistake of trying to figure out why your parents were like this. Why they did this to you. Why they were not more loving, more caring, kinder, more approving and accepting of you. Remember, they had their own set of parents who were probably not as ideal as they could have been, and so on, for as far back in your family history as you care to go. So *why* this all happened is not nearly as important as understanding that simply by realizing it happened and that it has colored your adult relationships (not only your love relationships, but possibly some of your friendships as well) - and certainly also your relationship with your children - *you now stand on the threshold of changing it, or changing yourself, and in the process of so doing, gaining immeasurable freedom.*

So having seen now how some of these patterns arise in our personalities, let's examine a few specific types of relationship patterns that we fall into. And in case you don't know, Carl Gustav Jung, who along with Sigmund Freud was one of the most renowned figures in the early annals of psychoanalysis, said that it is precisely the infinite intelligence of the psyche (in its quest to toward individuation and wholeness) that leads us to become attracted to certain individuals.

These individuals, as indicated above, will enable us to re-enact our childhood parental dynamics and scenarios that will more often than not - if we are paying attention - lead us to feel physical sensations in our body (e.g., clenching in the gut, a pounding heart, nausea, etc.) as well as to feel emotions that are strangely *familiar* to us. And of course the reason they are familiar is because we have felt them all before, when we were small. And that, by the way, is also the reason why our reactions in those situations are often the reactions of a child. *Not* because we are childish, but because this specific part of us has never grown or matured emotionally and psychologically; it remained arrested at that stage of development. But it *can mature* and - the more conscious and aware we become, *it will* indeed do so). This attraction to certain individuals that then leads to a relationship, may then - eventually - due to the later frustration and possible pain these individuals may bring to our lives (and we to theirs) ultimately offer us the opportunity to come to understanding and growth. This always leads to greater inner freedom.

PATTERNS:

Take Care of Me (Let Me Take Care of You!), AKA Poor Boundaries & Co-Dependence

It seems that as long as we remain unaware and unconscious in our lives, there is always a price to pay in our relationships. A woman may fall into the figurative lap of a man who offers to take care of her on some level (and it need not necessarily be financial, as the components of the caring he provides could be emotional or psychological, perhaps academic, professional or even social and spiritual). If she lies back, releasing a great sigh of relief, and allows him to do so, she almost always immediately relinquishes a part of her autonomy. It seems to be part of the *deal*, or simply the way the process works - subconsciously - for both partners.

In relinquishing part of her autonomy, she sets herself up to have her boundaries overstepped on some level. Perhaps the partner demands that in return she be there for him at all times, which precludes having a career of her own. Or he may demand she follow in his chosen field of academics, research, law or business, but in *his* footsteps, and not in those of her own making. This may lead to resentment and bitterness which may eventually erode the relationship, and/or the health of both partners. But it has its roots in the early relationship each of these partners had with their parents. One partner being cared for, acquiescing in some fashion, but paying a cruel price due to a fundamental lack of independence, and the other partner feeling he is only truly loved and needed if his "way" of thinking or behaving is adhered to, and if not, it is considered an act of high treason and proof of a lack in the way he is loved.

Or perhaps - this is another sample case - one of the partners recognizes a potential addiction problem in the other at an early stage in the relationship and decides that she will 'cure' that person. She just *knows* she will be able to do so, and furthermore, she also just knows that once her partner sees how truly wonderful he is - the way *she* sees him - then he will be able to begin to live out, in fact, the magnificence of his life and purpose. (All of this is possible, by the way, just not likely - at least not before these individuals begin to recognize that they are repeating a pattern). So here we have co-dependence rearing its ugly head, as well as, just like in the previous example, boundaries being overstepped, especially once the addicted person lets loose on their substance of choice.

And remember: if *your* boundaries are being crossed by your *partner*, it is *not* first and foremost your partner's fault, although he/she does carry responsibility. It is *your* responsibility to ensure that your own boundaries are healthy. And as long as you are enabling someone in a co-dependent relationship (by covering up the tracks - perhaps so that no one in your social circle notices - of a drinking or substance-smoking partner, for example, instead of setting some firm consequences if they do not clean up their act and then following through on those consequences), you are certainly not setting up healthy boundaries for yourself. This will affect your health, your state of mind, and last, but not least, the health of the relationship. And if this is not your first partnership of this type, but you're still behaving in this fashion, it is probably because you may not yet have recognized the pattern, and may be thinking instead: *why do I have such bad luck in choosing my partners?*

But here, once again, you are reliving some element of your past. Perhaps one of your parents him or herself was an addict of some kind, even if *only* workaholic, shopaholic, or experienced eating issues. And perhaps you learned early on to cover up their tracks so that no one would notice. The die is cast. And until you recognize it in your relationship patterns, you will continue to revisit this dynamic in your relationships, even though at the beginning of each relationship you are so very convinced that *this time it is truly different.* Or perhaps one of your parents took care of you in such a wonderful way, doing everything for you, solving all your problems, doting on you - as long as you toed a certain line.

And remember: the reason we seek the repetition of a dynamic is *not* to feel what we felt the way we did as helpless or unloved or manipulated children, but to *resolve* those unresolved issues that linger from our childhood.

If - in the above examples that deal with poor boundaries - I now recognize that I tend to choose individuals who will step on my boundaries, and if I now consciously work on creating healthy boundaries, I may begin to attract another kind of individual into my life - or said in other words - I may begin to be attracted to another kind of individual, and yet, my future relationships, while they will in all probability have *another* - difficult - kind of issue to work on, will nevertheless have progressed beyond *this* particular one, freeing me up enormously on those inner levels that are so important to well-being and inner harmony.

You will find additional material on the invariably deep-rooted subject of boundaries in other sections of this book.

Victim-Savior

This pattern is rather easy to understand, although less so when you are immersed in the middle of living out the scenario. If you are one of those very benevolent and generous individuals who spends a good portion of your time helping and giving to others, we speak well of you. We admire you. We believe you are a person to emulate. And perhaps you are. But perhaps not.

When you help others and give to others, there are a number of potential scenarios that can occur. Imagine a mentor, who furthers his protégé's knowledge about their mutually chosen field of endeavor. It's possible that the protégé may eventually outrun or surpass his mentor, and in so doing, obviously becomes autonomous at the very least, and possibly may find his mentor is no longer necessary to his growth. (Note: this doesn't mean that the protégé breaks off the relationship, but that the protégé will now want to be on a more equal footing with the mentor). At this point some mentors become very angry and feel betrayed, while others *feel gratified*. I give you one guess to decide which of these two has done some work on himself, has therefore grown, and is aware of himself.

Or imagine helping someone who is new in town. Showing them around, introducing them to all your friends, helping them find a place to live and then a job. And then, perhaps later when they are more established, you discover that they have organized a party and invited most of those people you introduced them to, *but did not invite you*. At this point you may become very angry and feel betrayed, or you may feel very despondent. Either way, clearly this is not how a person whom we admire for their generosity in helping others should feel. In other words: when you help others and give to others, you need to be very clear inside yourself about *exactly why* you are giving and helping, and if it has more to do with how good you feel when others feel thankful and perhaps even beholden or obligated to you, then you will need to examine your motivations very carefully indeed. (While it is also true that not inviting you to the party seems inconsiderate, unkind, or rude given the circumstances, remember that this is *not* about the other person but about what you can see or recognize in yourself due to your interaction with someone.)

Let's take the examples a bit closer into the love relationship arena. You meet someone who is not making ends meet. You believe they've had a rough deal in life so far. You take them under your wing. In the process, you fall in love. You cherish this person (and I've seen this example in both genders, i.e., sometimes the person who had a rough deal is the woman, and sometimes it is the man). You take care of him/her in all senses of the word. You pay for furthering his/her education, you pay for a better wardrobe (also in part so that you can feel good about him/her when you are seen together), and eventually you get married. You want to make your partner feel equal to you in all things, so you open a joint bank account, and when you buy a house, you put half in your partner's name. You have some children, and so of course your partner doesn't really ever have time to pursue a career, if she is the wife, and if it's the husband who had the rough life prior to meeting you, clearly it is possible that you are the one who continues working directly after giving birth, and your husband may stay home with the baby. You can see where this is going. At some point your partner either makes more and more demands while giving less and less, and you begin to believe you have been used, and want to break away from the relationship yourself, or your partner announces out of the blue that he/she wants a divorce and before you know it, you are served papers that show that you are going to be taken to the cleaners and that your children may even be wrested from you. You are in shock. You feel enormous rage and outrage. You feel betrayed. And you feel deep sadness. Not at all the way someone who started out being kind, generous and helpful should ultimately feel, right?

But let's examine what happened in the examples I've offered where the 'generous' person wound up feeling angry and betrayed. Could we say that he 'saved' the other person from having to do something on their own? Could it be that he saved the other person from standing on their own two feet? Or could it be that he did it, not because he was so generous and helpful (at least not in the first instance), but because of *how good it makes him feel* to have another be grateful to him? Or to admire him for his skills and abilities, or social contacts, or ease at accomplishing things?

Let's take that one step further: while it is true that at the beginning the gratitude and even admiration the other person shows you is authentic, it is also true that after a time it may pall. Perhaps he/she now wishes to strike out on his own but feels stymied by your need to be needed in this particular way. Or perhaps he becomes resentful of your 'power' over him. That could be financial, social, academic, professional, and so on. Either way, he/she is no longer happy to be with you, and definitely not with your demands, unspoken or otherwise, to be kept up on a pedestal. And so the savior, who has rescued the victim, is abandoned, shunned or otherwise cast off.

But where did this relationship pattern come from? As a child you may have unwittingly and unwillingly been cast into the savior role: a role that should never be foisted upon anyone, least of all on an unsuspecting and helpless child that - in true child-like fashion - merely yearns to be loved. You might be the little girl who takes on many of mommy's duties because she is too tired or irresponsible herself. You might be the little boy who became mommy's 'little helper' and whom she admired so much, as long as you did exactly what she expected of you. You felt the brunt of her disapproval when you were not there for her in the way she expected, and because it was never resolved (most probably because you never truly understood the dynamics of the role that had been thrust on you by an adult who herself refused to be an adult and expected you to take that on), you have (your *psyche* has) the need - albeit subconscious - to relive this particular drama until you get the reaction of full-time love, admiration and approval that you craved as a child.

Evidently that does not happen in the adult pattern repetition, at least not ultimately, and therefore you are literally forced to seek another solution. And that *lies within you* and not in the other person's approval of you. But you won't understand that until you have undergone the process and begun to work it out.

The other way this pattern can work is that you are the victim. You were always 'saved' as a child by your parent or parents. When you got into scrapes, or when you broke the neighbor's window with your baseball, or shoplifted adult magazines from the store, and were found out, your parent covered for you. Or paid someone off. Or made excuses for you. Or you bullied someone at school and your parent 'fixed' it. Or maybe you couldn't get into college, but your parent had a friend on the board and you scraped by with your not-so-outstanding grades and got in thanks to that connection. Whatever happened, you learned to rely on another to get you through. And now this other - perhaps your wife or husband - has had enough of you not pulling your own weight. And so they leave you. And you find yourself another savior or rescuer. And after a time it happens again. And you are beginning to glimpse the possibility that there may be a pattern. Because of course what you need to learn is to find the wherewithal in *you* to resolve your problems, as opposed to getting another to do it for you.

Please Love Me & Never Leave Me / *Don't* Suffocate Me: The Paradox of Neediness & Emotional Unavailability

In this pattern dynamic we find couples that come together because they *depend* on each other, although at first glance one is the dependent partner and the other is the *independent* partner. Yet, after careful examination, we come to the conclusion that they both depend on each other very deeply for very similar reasons:

they represent two sides of one single coin, although it may take them a great deal of time to fully capture the essence of this idea.

The more obviously dependent partner is clearly needy, mostly in the emotional sense, although it may also be in other ways. Emotional neediness basically means that the partner believes he or she is unable to live without the love of the apparently more independent partner. It means he believes that he is not sufficient for his own well-being. It means he has not learned to love himself. It means - and this is the most important aspect of it - he/she will do *anything* at all in order to ensure the continuation of the love of the partner that is considered so necessary for his/her well-being.

An external need, in others words, when we depend on something *external* to ourselves for our well-being, frequently carries within it the seeds of failure. In the case of a relationship, it may often be the cause of power plays between the two people, the less *needy* one being the one to dominate the relationship, and the *needier* one to resentfully accept this dominance due to his or her need for the other partner.

Power plays are not the only manifestation of relationships mired in mutual need. Another frequent expression is obsession or possessiveness, or a need to control. And you can imagine – if you haven't been there – the kind of resentment and negative feelings that this can generate on the part of both people is massive. Akin to any substance addiction, obsession or possessiveness or the need to control can take people to hellish places in their hearts and minds that few of us would wish to visit. I have created an entire workshop on this topic, because although this type of addiction is often masked by a veneer of sophistication, it occurs more frequently than most people suspect, and makes the existence of those that suffer from it a living nightmare. (You will find more about this subject later in this chapter).

So why do we become needy in relationships? Of the roughly 40% men and 60% women that I see in my private practice, many would initially answer that 'needing' your love partner is how it should be. But why should love imply a feeling that almost always develops into something negative, and at best, makes those who feel it believe that they could not live without the beloved, thus 'proving' in their minds, that this is really love? Is that really what love is all about?

Wouldn't it make more sense to assume that love means freedom rather than independence? What does needing our partner tell us?

Let's start with the falling in love part. What are we actually falling in love with? Stated simply, we fall in love with those bits and pieces of *ourselves* that we have not yet recognized, but that we find (via projection) in the partner. Is she tender and understanding? Is he funny and the center of the party? Is she strong and enterprising? Is he confident, with a great sense of integrity? All of those qualities may well be part of your partner's character, but the fact that you fell in love with those specific traits, tells you that they are actually part of your own character *as well*.

Since you probably do not yet manifest those qualities, because you have not yet recognized them in yourself, you need your partner to be able to 'be in touch with' that part of you. That is what 'hooks' you on your partner. Your partner's presence in your life gives you contact to those parts of you that you have not yet developed, making you feel in some unmistakable way that your partner is absolutely indispensable to your well-being.

So then, when something happens to the relationship, or your partner leaves, or threatens to leave, the strong feelings of need arise. It often happens long before that, when you are apart during the workday, or when one of the two is away on business, and you notice how much you *need* the other's presence for that wonderful sense of well-being you so crave. This is the time when you should realize that these strong feelings of need are a vast red flag letting you know something is going on inside of you *that only you can do something about*. If you ignore it, or initially translate it into: *"Because I need him/her so much, I just know this is true love"* and then later: *"I was deeply wounded by my partner"*, or *"my partner did not return my feelings when I most needed him/her, so I guess that means I always choose the wrong people"*, or *"next time I will choose better, so that this kind of thing never happens to me again"*, then instead of resolving your inner dilemma, you will merely perpetuate it by maintaining the status quo inside of you, falling in love with yet another person that puts you in touch with bits of you that you have not yet recognized in yourself, and thus setting yourself up to be 'needy'.

So what is the solution? Simple to state, less simple to execute (mainly because it requires some of that inner discipline that most of us don't want to exercise): work on those bits of yourself that *you catch a glimpse of* in the beloved. Examine yourself to see where they might reside in you. Work at developing them; growing them, and become proactive about learning how to fulfill your own needs. Also challenge yourself to always finding inner balance and a measure of well-being, *no matter what the outer circumstances*. Doing this gets you on the road to freedom from needing another or the presence of another for you to feel good. *This literally signifies that you will be learning to love yourself.* If you do this, I guarantee you that the next time you fall in love, it will be with a smaller degree of external need, and hence, a greater degree of internal freedom. Or, if you remain with the same person, your love will grow into something infinitely more loving.

The other side of the coin in this particular relationship pattern is emotional unavailability. Emotional unavailability can be devastating to everyone touched by it. People often mistakenly understand it as a ploy on the part of the emotionally unavailable person to *use* others, or to *get without giving*, and while it is true that some of that may happen at times, it is also true that it consistently undermines the existence of the one who suffers from it, and consequently wraps its painful tentacles around those who are in the life of that person.

It's a subject fraught with pain and difficulty, potentially more so for the person on the receiving end of an emotionally unavailable partner, parent, or friend, but also on the side of the individual who "plays" out the role of the emotionally unavailable person, as they too, as stated, can suffer tremendously from it.

How can we define the emotionally unavailable person? These are individuals who are:

- cut off from their own emotions and emotional processes
- cut off from others' emotions as well as their emotional processes
- very disconnected from the emotional content of their lives

Let's take a closer look at all of these points.

Cut Off From Their Own Emotional Processes:

Imagine that a friend or a partner abandons you, either out of the blue, or after an argument, and has now disappeared from your life. Imagine that you feel that you did not deserve such treatment. Clearly, you would experience hurt, disappointment, frustration, pain, sorrow, and so on. You might also feel angry and indignant.

The emotionally unavailable person, however, would not only *not* acknowledge the majority of these feelings, but would probably insist that the whole thing is not really terribly important, or that it was just as well that it happened. In other words, they would have little recognition of these feelings swirling around inside of them. They might complain of gastric upset, or a headache, or back pain, or knee discomfort, or unexplained difficulties in walking, or any other manifestation that shows that the process went into their body due to it not being acknowledged on the emotional level.

On the other hand, if this person has begun a relationship with someone, and they notice that they are thinking about the other person a lot, and that they enjoy spending time with the other person, and that somehow the sun shines more brightly when they are around the other person, they would not interpret this as the beginning of love, the way many other individuals might, but would perhaps say, after a brief time of enjoying the "warm sunshine" of the other's presence: *you're crowding me*, or *I need more space*, or *we need to cool it for a while*, or *I don't know how you do it, but you're really maneuvering yourself into my life*, or *this is going too quickly for me*, or simply *I really don't want a relationship*, or *I always said I didn't want a commitment* (and note that they may often marry or cohabit, but although they share bed and house, they *rarely share themselves*.)

Clearly, the emotionally unavailable person is saying this *because they are beginning to feel discomfort in the presence of the other because they are unable to handle the surge of their own emotions in connection to the other person.* This is not conscious, nor is this done or said from a position of nastiness or miserliness, much that it may often appear to be that. This is, in fact, most generally a defense mechanism learned, in all likelihood in childhood, to safeguard the child against hurt from people he/she had loved and who somehow drastically let him down. *Sometimes this letting down happens* only *in the perception of the child.*

Early childhood attachment studies (Ainsworth & Bell, 1970) indicate that abandonment by the parents, and particularly by the mother, creates much greater problems with later emotional availability than even physical abuse. Abandonment, logically, does not only mean a totally absent parent, but also a parent who disappears for a period of time in the early life of the infant (especially during the first 12-18 months of life), such as those children whose parents must leave them in hospital, or some kind of institution and are not able to visit frequently.

Nevertheless, the experience, whether it truly happened, or was only perceived, or happened for totally innocent reasons (the child's life had to be saved by hospitalizing it) carries enormous weight in the adult and with his/her relationships with persons of the opposite sex (or the same gender in gay relationships.)

Cut Off From Others' Emotional Processes:

It follows that the emotionally unavailable person has not a clue about the state of another person's emotions, *even when faced with that person's tears or recriminations, or pain, which may be totally evident to others, but not necessarily to the emotionally unavailable person.* In the face of these emotions in the other person, the emotionally unavailable person often feels put upon, burdened with an onerous duty, that he or she mainly wants to escape from, because it feels far too heavy, and heavy often feels dangerous. That makes for a very difficult relationship, to say the least.

Disconnected From the Emotional Content of Their Lives:

Despite the disconnection from the emotional content of their lives, emotionally unavailable persons might be connected to bits of it with those people they do not feel threatened by. For example: they may be very loving and tender to children - especially the very young children - of other people, or very caring and tender to other people's partners (in the right way, not in the wrong way, i.e. as good and supportive friends). Or they may have a deeply caring relationship with a pet, or be very much into caring for plants, gardening, and so on.

But the conscious and self-reflective connection to their own emotional content is generally non-existent.

I repeat, emotional unavailability tends not to be conscious. The emotionally unavailable person spends an enormous amount of psychological energy maintaining the "wolves at bay". In order not to have to deal with their own emotions, their defense mechanisms have become automatic, and spring up, the way a bridge over a castle moat springs up against the castle walls to prevent intruders from approaching too closely. (For more about what I am calling the *moat syndrome* see Chapter 5).

It is only when this process becomes conscious, that the emotionally unavailable person is in a position to do something about it, and this person may fight tooth and nail in order to *not become aware*. They may insist that they don't want to leave their comfort zone, or that they never wanted a commitment, and shrug their shoulders and leave it at that, never having come any closer to a conscious realization of their inner scarring and crippled heart and spirit.

Often - but not always - the emotionally unavailable person is also unavailable sexually, or, if they have made some outward commitment, such as sharing a home, or having a child with the partner, they may withdraw emotionally and sexually, finding it far too emotionally taxing to be engaged on more than one level - in this case, simply living together is enough. Becoming distant from one's partner or not being sexually responsive are also ways of cutting off genuine relating.

So what does emotional unavailability tell you about *you* if you are with an emotionally unavailable partner? And how can you deal with it?

There have probably been issues with the parents and unmet or disappointed emotions on your part, leaving you feeling bereft and alone, like an abandoned child. You may have learned a dysfunctional model of love, where love was never freely given. This in turn may have created a deep well of neediness, neediness,

neediness, and more neediness, which in turn caused you to have a lack of boundaries - *please step all over me, just as long as you love me*. This is implicit in a lack of self-respect, self-worth, self-love, etc., and there tends to be a desire to fuse or merge with a new partner almost immediately. Frequently there is a loss of identity, and of course one tends to be addicted to the partner which implies withdrawal symptoms of the worst kind if and when the partner leaves.

This process is also unconscious. What the person with this aspect of dysfunctionality is aware of, is the pain. But he or she interprets the pain as the fault of *the partner, the emotionally unavailable partner, because he/she is not behaving the way this person would like him to behave. Consequently, blame is placed firmly on the shoulders of the emotionally unavailable person by the partner who is not getting what he wants, and hence this partner does not become aware of his own need to clear up the issue of neediness, lack of boundaries, lack of real meaning in the life, and above all, the lack of self-love that everything else points to.*

Whether the emotionally unavailable person is behaving "properly" or not from an emotional point of view, is actually not the point, because it is *not a question of "fixing"* the emotionally unavailable partner. Yes, it *is* true that those issues need to be worked on, but it is also the partner who feels rejected or feels that the other is cold and unemotional, who needs to *take a good look at the reasons he or she is attracted over and over again into situations of this nature.* It may mean, that as you work on yourself in order to resolve these issues, you may need *to get out of the relationship, and get out fast!* Conversely, you may need to be very kind to yourself if you are unable - at this point - to leave your cold partner and recognize that the process of learning to love yourself may take some time and that only when those "muscles" are strong enough, you will, in fact, be able to become proactive about leaving if your partner any interest in being more emotionally available.

Now to understand why neediness and emotional unavailability are two sides of the same coin, recognize that both are based on a *lack* of self love. Both are based as well on *fear* of love and the hurt that love can engender due to the vulnerability that being in love generally evokes. Precisely because of this, it frequently happens that one person may live out one side of the coin (neediness) in several relationships and then - in a totally different relationship - may find him or herself living out the other side of the coin (emotional unavailability).

Looking For Daddy (or Mommy)

This one can work in several ways. You might not have had *enough* of your opposite gender parent as a child. Or you might have had too much, in the sense of being over-protected, over-loved, over-spoiled. Either way, it was dysfunctional, and you will seek - subconsciously - to correct the dysfunction by repeating the pattern with your adult partners. As long as they play the role you were accustomed as a child, nothing changes. But if they should leave you, or if you, by any chance, decide that not being loved properly (in the case where you are repeating the pattern of a missing, absent or rejecting father or mother, for example) is not good, and hence *you*, yourself, are in fact the one who leaves, you will initially crave another relationship that allows you to work out the pattern, and so you will assume you have chosen badly, or had bad luck in your initial choice of partner. However, as already stated repeatedly in this chapter, once you recognize that there is a pattern (after several such failed relationships), you may begin to sit up and take notice.

In the example of little girls who live without a father, we find that they do so not only due to death, abandonment, or divorce, but also *despite* a physically present father who may be emotionally absent, or ill over a lengthy period of time in some way (clinical depression, terminal disease, etc.), or because the father is a workaholic, or occasionally because in some fashion the father is a disappointment to the daughter, as might be the case in a weak or ineffectual father. Such differing types of absence in the girl's life may have major consequences of varying kinds, since a healthy emotional and socio-psychological developmental trajectory in the early years of life *does* require some type of positive paternal role model.

Optimally, a little girl needs to see herself reflected in the love she sees in her father's eyes. This is how she develops self-confidence and self-esteem. This is how she develops a healthy familiarity with what a positive expression of love feels like. This is how she develops an appreciation for her own looks, her own body and her entire way of being. This is how she develops what Jungians would call her "animus", her counter-sexual self; her masculine self, which will help her be proactive, productive, and creative in the outer world as she grows into adulthood.

If, however, the little girl does *not* have such a relationship with the father, if she sees rejection or emotional coldness or withdrawal in him, or if he simply is not available at all, her sense of self will be tainted, her self-confidence warped or non-existent, her portrait of a loving relationship may be distorted or dysfunctional, and she may find herself, no matter how pretty, vivacious, lovable, funny, or intelligent, lacking in appeal.

Clearly, self-confidence and self-esteem can be forged through one's own endeavors during the life course, even if a father has not been present, but the path to success in such endeavors, and the *reasons* for which they are even attempted, tend to be quite different in the adult woman who was raised with a positive relationship to her father, as opposed to the one who was not. The former may excel simply because she believes in herself, while the latter *needs* to excel in order to catch a glimpse of approval and recognition in the eyes of those who give her a message of approval, honor, or prestige. The value of such a belief in oneself, easily acquired by the woman with a positive relationship to her father, is immeasurable in the adult life, and the lack of it in many of the countless women who were raised without a positive father image, may cause the life course to be fraught with difficulties *until conscious understanding allows growth out of this warped tunnel to take place.*

Perhaps the arena in which the most painful process of learning how to deal with the early lack of a father is played out is in that of relationships. If a girl has not been assured of her value as a woman by that early relationship with the father, she finds it difficult to relate to men precisely because she may often unconsciously seek to find that recognition in the eyes of the beloved and this may lead her down an early path of promiscuity, which in turn makes her feel she is not a "good" girl, but on she marches, relentlessly visiting bed after bed, locking in fierce embrace with man after man, in the hope that *this* one or *that* one, or the *next* one will finally give her that which she never had as a child – validation of herself *for herself.*

Other women may choose another route, falling in love with an older man and thus marrying "daddy". At this point many different scenarios may ensue. If the man is at all psychologically aware (something often, but not always lacking in older men who like younger girls), he may have a vague inkling of what is going on. Therefore, once she starts – within the secure confines of the relationship or marriage – the process of growth, which will inevitably lead her to separate from her husband in some ways that are emotionally and psychologically necessary in order for her become her own woman, he will not blanch in fear at this process, and allow her the necessary space and freedom to do so. In that case, the marriage will in all likelihood thrive and continue to grow. If, however, the man is not aware, and sees her search for growth as a threat to the superiority he felt upon marrying a young, and as yet undeveloped woman, he will attempt to stifle her, to manipulate her psychologically by making her believe she is worthless, silly, or, and this appears to be a perennial favorite, that she "needs professional help in order to calm down and behave like she used to before".

Another possible scenario (and there are many more which for reasons of space cannot be touched upon here) is that of avoiding relationships entirely, or *of avoiding the engagement of one's emotions.* Examples abound: the maiden aunt, who dedicates her life to her nieces and nephews, or who becomes a teacher and dedicates her life to her career; the nun, who dedicates her life to God, or the prostitute, who, although she may engage her body, rarely engages her emotions. Another example is that of the eternal seductress, who needs to remain in control by seducing the man and never actually involving her own feelings. A slightly more difficult to recognize version of the same scenario is played out by the woman who consistently has relationships with married men who never leave their respective wives for her. On an unconscious level this suits her just fine because it gives her the perfect excuse never to have to commit herself totally.

The core of the matter is, of course, that the self-confidence and recognition so avidly sought must be found within oneself rather than in the outer world - at least initially - in order to be of lasting and true value. The world of emotions that is avoided out of fear or because one never really learned what love is, must first be found in oneself (i.e., it is necessary to love the self *before* one loves another). The task of accomplishing this, requires that the individual become aware of him or herself (by observing the self, the *self-talk*, and all emotions that occur, good or bad, since all of these serve to give clues about the true self), and that *absolute honesty* about oneself be employed in this process. Let the reader be warned: this process is not a simple weekend project; it must be ongoing throughout life; it must become second nature, but it will pave the road to finding inner self-confidence and love for oneself, which will in turn lead to the eradication of the need for finding these things in another. This is one of the roads to inner freedom that psychological knowledge and spiritual understanding offers.

Obsession, Possession & Control

As we've already seen, every single relationship begins with a projection, even though we understand it as love, chemistry, infatuation, and under the guise of many other names. This applies even to people who are totally aware and conscious, but the difference is that they will recognize the projection very quickly and from that position of awareness, will then decide what to do about their burgeoning attraction to the other. However, when we aren't at that aware state yet, because of the nature of projections, where we often feel very attracted or repelled for reasons that at the beginning seem very clear, such as something you very much "love" about the other person, or something you very much "dislike", it typically signifies that those relationships in which we do find ourselves strongly attracted to someone quite quickly, in a way that goes beyond the mere physical or chemical attraction, we are almost certainly involved in a projection of our own psyche. *Therefore* - at least until we start becoming aware and begin a growth process - *most relationships of a close nature that we embark upon tie into something that was important in our childhood.*

We tend to seek the familiar which we find in our early childhood patterns that set the pace for future relationships, until we discover the patterns and sort them out. Here are some more patterns (but by no means all) that lead to adult relationships we enter with the subconscious goal of attempting to resolve them:

My father/mother tended to:

- ignore me
- pay continual attention to me
- reject me
- criticize me
- praise me no matter what I did
- judge me
- belittle me
- make fun of me
- make me believe I was unique and special compared to other, more 'ordinary' kids
- show me off to his/her friends
- leave me alone for long periods
- smother me with attention
- say that things were always my fault
- say that things were never my fault
- say that I was the responsible one
- say that I did not have to be responsible because it was someone else's fault
- make sure I realized it was better not to speak up
- make sure I realized it was best to always keep the peace
- make sure I realized it was best to always try to make everyone feel good

As stated at the beginning of this chapter, until we discover and recognize our patterns, we are attracted to precisely those individuals who will live out the pattern for us, or with whom we can re-live the pattern because it serves the purpose of making us come closer to knowing ourselves and in that knowing, we come closer to being psychologically free. Nevertheless, at the point at which the attraction happens, we're generally not aware of this in the least. All we know is that we are attracted to someone, and if we tend to be obsessive and if we have found ourselves in previous relationships that began like this, we may also be aware of the fact that when we actually get into these relationships, we are *not free*. (Humanistic astrology – as opposed to predictive astrology – is excellent at picking up on these patterns of relationships upon careful examination of the cross-aspects between the charts of the two people.)

In this painful neediness that shows up as either trying to control others in an effort to assure yourself of their love, or allowing yourself to be controlled by others, in an effort to make sure that they will continue to love you, there might be a strongly-etched underlying lack of self-esteem. All of this makes for extremely difficult relationships. Here are some characteristics of people who confuse love with obsession, and who therefore believe that because they feel or do any of the following, it means that they are in love:

- They can't get a love interest out of their mind - no matter how hard they try.
- They seek self-validation through a love interest or relationship.
- They may use sex, emotions and even food to exact control over another.
- They try to control a partner using emotional or psychological abuse.
- They check up on a partner or make a loved one continually account for their whereabouts.
- They may go into debt trying to find or keep love or the *illusion* of love.
- They may stalk, harass or even become violent towards a partner.
- They obsess over a partner, trying to control him/her at any cost.

What love really is remains much of a mystery to many of us. Its very enigmatic nature is what often spurs us on in the quest to find that elusive pot of gold at the end of the rainbow that we aspire to. Our intentions tend to be good, and we are basically almost all aware of the fact that love can have different faces at different moments of a relationship. However obsession is not at all the same; it is a destructive form of love that needs understanding and avoiding. Key to this understanding whether you are in love or obsessed with someone and vice versa is this: when you are obsessed you find it nearly impossible to function as a person on a daily basis without thinking about the other. If *you* are the one who is obsessed, you focus on getting all the attention from your partner, or if it is your partner who is obsessed, he/she aims at getting all *your* attention. The one who obsesses will make it difficult or, at the very least, uncomfortable in some fashion, for the other to keep in normal touch with friends and family because when people confuse love with obsession, they will do nearly anything to keep the "love object" a figurative prisoner and locked up in the relationship. When you love, however, there is mutual support, caring and giving. Healthy love is the opposite of controlling.

The following suggestions may serve as a guide to allow you to see more clearly and begin to resolve your patterns of obsession:

- Identify how you attempt to control others (e.g., emotional, sexual, financial manipulation, etc.) This requires great self-honesty and awareness.
- Forgive others.
- Forgive yourself.
- Attempt to understand your childhood patterns.
  - Exercises for doing this:
    - Analyze your relationships, search for patterns by examining how it was when you fell in love and what caused the demise of each relationship.
    - Imagine your ideal partner - write down reasons why you are attracted to this type of person and try to understand why. Is it related to what you feel is missing in you? What can you do to fill that missing element yourself, as opposed to filling it with an ideal partner?

- Identify how you are soothing yourself. These self-medicating mechanisms will contribute to your need to control.
    - For people who confuse love with obsession, it is common to struggle with some kind of addiction. In order to cope with your pain (or to run from it), you may have learned to soothe yourself with any number of not-so-healthy mechanisms, including, but not restricted to alcohol, drugs, food, and/or sex, shopping, and gambling. This may apply most particularly during difficult times, when an object of obsession causes you to experience anxiety or emotional distress.
- Self-talk: what messages are you giving yourself on a daily basis?
- Begin to have a relationship with yourself. Seek the inner connection:
    - By confusing love with obsession you are well on the road to becoming a stranger to yourself because you focus all your energy on the *other*, hoping to manipulate him/her into your desired modes of behavior. You may also continually obsess about the other's emotions, thoughts, acts, needs and happiness and leave your *own* to one side. Due to this need to control the other as well as the relationship, you wind up not cultivating the most important relationship of all – *a relationship with yourself.*
    - By focusing on your love for yourself and consciously creating a healthy relationship with yourself.
- Become aware and self-aware (emotions, body language, and inner energy).
- Realize - and then internalize it as a strong conviction - that you always have a choice.

Here is the biggest and most important thing you can do in this process of helping yourself – whether you are the one who confuses obsession with love, or whether you are the one whose partner is trying to control: *become aware of what is happening.* Don't blame the other. There is *never, never, never* any point in that. Understand that *both* of you are in this *dance* in order to release childhood patterns, throw away old (and very heavy) baggage, *in order to be able to grow in magnificent new directions.* There lie freedom, peace, and inner harmony.

****

There are numerous other patterns in relationships, and variations on those already described here. However, the purpose of this chapter is not to exhaust the possibilities, but merely point out that this - living out the patterns - is a phase in our relationship lives that occurs more often than not, and that the sooner we can recognize our particular pattern and understand its purpose in our lives, the sooner we will be able to move beyond it, and attract another kind of relationship. It goes without saying, as you can imagine, what I would wish and hope for you, is that the new relationship be a spiritual partnership in the sense that I will be discussing in this book.

Chapter 2

The Purpose of Relationships

As we have discussed, both historically and culturally, we have been lulled into numerous erroneous - and potentially harmful - beliefs regarding relationships. Such beliefs are harmful because of the enormous weight their psychological and emotional expectations bring to bear on us, that barely allow us to discern the more accurate, and in fact, the more *healthy* reality.

Society lies at the foundation of our belief in the idea that relationships owe us some degree of happiness and bliss ever after. Mass media encourage us to swallow these ideas from the day we begin to watch television, flip through magazines, see movies, read billboards and understand their meaning. We are raised on these premises, we genuflect to these ideas *because a part of us wants them to be so* and then evidently when reality intrudes, we are shocked, horrified, and devastated that happy-ever-after appears not to be as it was portrayed. While happy couples do exist, divorce statistics indicate a great majority simply is not happy after the first glow dims. A well-known Jungian quotation states: *Everything that irritates us about others can lead to an understanding of ourselves.*

Centuries before, Rumi wrote: *If you are irritated by every rub, how will your mirror be polished?*

Clients - highly intelligent and cosmopolitan clients - have informed me in hushed but adamant tones that *working on a relationship* is simply not something they are willing to do because if you have to work at it, they believe, it means the relationship was never meant to be, that it is doomed to failure, and that it proves there was never any *real* love to begin with. In other words, these are *not* lazy clients, who are unwilling to roll up their sleeves, but a spell of sorts has been cast on their powers of discernment in this arena; we might say they are bedazzled or bewitched individuals who bought into the fairy tale. Or - sometimes it's not so much that they bought into the fairy tale - but that they so desperately want the idea of *true love and happy every after* to be true. Often this occurs due to a challenging childhood. *At least in my love relationship*, they think - most often subconsciously - *I will have all that which I didn't get as a child*. Therefore as soon as it does not work, they feel they chose the partner badly, or were mistaken, because otherwise it would all run smoothly *with no work necessary*. After all, Prince Charming and Snow White did not have to do any relationship work, *did they*?

The fact, of course, that a good portion of the work required deals with becoming conscious of themselves and their various blind or hidden sides, escapes them at this point, and hence, very regrettably, often nothing is undertaken, and one more human being fails to wake up and thus does not begin to live a conscious life. The transformative offer of a difficult or failing relationship is frequently not accepted, and much growth potential is unwittingly thrown away and lost.

Relationship Transformation

Nevertheless, as much as it surprises many to hear this, it is *precisely* this less appealing reality of a relationship that does not work out the way the couple believed it would in their erstwhile honeymoon glow, which in fact holds the key for a true loving relationship that is *free of dependence on the other.* Jung wrote: *"The meeting of two personalities is like the contact of two chemical substances: if there is any reaction, both are transformed."* In a nutshell, *transformation* is what relationships are all about. We remain in relationships while the going is good, but often break off at the first sign of trouble. If the person we love turns out differently than our initial estimation of them, we feel they led us to believe something about their character that was not true, or, that we simply cannot trust our judgment, or that we had bad luck in our choice of partner and so on.

But if relationships are in fact about transformation and most people don't know this, or don't take it into consideration, or indeed, they may do so, but then decide they simply don't want the work it would involve (much of this work involving their own issues and how these impact on the relationship), then they lose one of the most brilliant opportunities for growth each time they give up on a relationship before at least having looked at it from this perspective. This is not a matter of crusading against divorce but a matter of encouraging you to look at what you are discarding and what it may be showing you about yourself.

This is the crux of the matter. It is precisely at this problematic point in the relationship that we are offered the opportunity to create a new foundation for it based on mutual complementarity rather than on need; a free relationship between two people who *want* to be together, rather than two people who *need* to be together. We can begin to 'grow' a relationship that serves a much higher purpose than making us happy, although being happy most certainly *also* forms part of it. The higher purpose, of course, is the path - the *tao* - to transformation and growth, not only psychologically and emotionally, but also spiritually through our gradual acceptance that each and every stumbling block of the relationship contains within it in seed form the possibility of leading us closer to our own self and in so doing, of leading us closer and connecting us to our partner in ways that those who simply have only known the "honeymoon" variety of relationships, can merely dream of.

Why, you ask, *would we want to be together if things have gone from bad to worse?* If you could, just for a moment, *imagine* that by undergoing a process of coming to consciousness, of getting to know yourself and love yourself in ways you never have, of literally transforming the way you have known yourself thus far, and *imagine* as well, that your partner were doing the same, and that then, the two of you from this new perspective of greater self-understanding and immense love of self were to *relate* to each other in new ways that would raise your relationship to levels you had never even dreamed of, not even during the honeymoon phase, would you not want to give it a shot? Granted, it's not instant coffee, if that's what you're after, but deep, rich espresso that delivers flavor and punch the instant kind could never do. And just as espresso requires greater preparation and more work to produce than instant anything, so does a relationship of the type I'm describing, require greater preparation and more work. Above all, it requires greater consciousness.

Obviously the preparation is not something you will have done *prior* to getting into a relationship, if this is the first time you're hearing about the concept, and are, indeed, in the middle - or at the tail end - of a swiftly declining relationship. So preparation means what you do now, at this moment, when all that stuff has already hit the fan and you were - perhaps - ready to throw in the towel.

So how do you get there? How do you proceed? What steps can you take?

A very important step in this process is becoming aware of the self; gaining insight into the self. Another big step is learning to love the self. I wrote an entire book about these topics and since this book that you are holding in your hands concerns spiritual - or growth - partnerships, I suggest, if you need additional clarity in the area of gaining insight into the self and of loving the self, that you take a look at that earlier book *Rewiring the Soul*. You will also learn more about both topics here in Chapter 3.

Fulfilling Your Own Needs

A further step involves filling our lagunae, our own "holes", our needs, rather than hoping to fill them through others. Clearly this is easier said than done. *It literally means growing into wholeness* - a lifelong process - but the good news is that you can start *right now* and that you can make a difference right now, the moment that you start! The beginning of all of this is understanding that one of the greatest needs we have is that of being loved. But we first have to fulfill this need ourselves by loving ourselves. If we do not do this, our *need for love* gets us into all the difficult relationship entanglements being discussed here because we didn't begin by first supplying love *for* ourselves *from* ourselves.

We seek out people, consciously or unconsciously, that fulfill our needs, rather than filling our needs ourselves. Whenever we obsess about someone, feeling that we cannot live without them, we should examine *what* it is that is missing in us very carefully, *what* we feel others are "giving" us, and *why* we feel that we need them for our very survival. This element is being shown to us through the relationship, the obsession, the need, the desire to control and possess. And again, it's also being shown to us through the *need* to be loved. Please don't misunderstand - we all *want* to be loved, but once we *need a particular person to love us*, things begin to look very different, and may perhaps become quite unhealthy and dysfunctional.

If my love for myself is healthy, if I know that I will maintain inner balance and peace, no matter what happens, even if my circumstances change drastically and life becomes very difficult indeed, then I will be in such a good place inside myself that while I will *enjoy* being in a loving relationship, and while I will *thrive* in a loving relationship, I *know* that I will neither fall apart nor become needy, desperate, depressed or even suicidal if my partner leaves me. But of course, if I have not yet realized all of this, and therefore am not living my life that way, then my love relationships may potentially bring me great suffering because of my *perceived need* in the unhealthy way described, for my partner.

One of the main reasons we *need* others, or a *specific other* to love us is because of what was touched upon in the chapter on patterns: we were left longing for love and acceptance as children. We were left longing for that feeling of safety and security that a child who is raised in a healthy adult environment simply has. But of course so many of us did *not* have that because our parents were not healthy adults, because - once again - they themselves were not raised in such an environment. (Do you begin to understand the magnitude of repercussions there would be, if you were to bring yourself to a level of what I am calling being a healthy adult? It would not only change your life but would impact on your partner's life, on that of your children, and their children's children *because your children would not grow up with issues similar to yours.* You would have given them a different psychological and emotional legacy - not to mention the potential spiritual ramifications.) So if as a child you were left with a longing for love, which to some seems like a bottomless well, then obviously when you find someone who initially loves you, or shows you love and acceptance, and you revel in the joy that such love and acceptance makes you feel, then you will fall into a trap of your psycho-emotional background's making, where you now *need* that person to feel good. All you are thinking is that when you are with that person you feel good, and when you are not, you don't feel as good or perhaps not good at all. And so it begins.

Part of it, of course, is also due to our socialization; mass media that tell us that when we need someone it means that we love them. Needing, they say, is the measure of love, but for a fully conscious individual *nothing could be further from the truth.* And therein lies part of the secret of spiritual partnerships.

Loving the Self

If we could only become aware of all of these possible scenarios, we might still suffer, but we would have finally found the real road to freedom from this kind of dependent need for another individual. If we could only understand that such need signifies incompleteness and that the more complete we are, the freer we are to enter a relationship on a totally different basis, a relationship without the constraints of a prison fashioned by our clamoring need that has its roots in our childhood and in not having learned to love ourselves first.

As stated, self-love is one of those foundational topics I wrote about in *Rewiring the Soul* so I won't delve too deeply into the subject here except to say *lack of self-love and not understanding the need for self-love* is one of the greatest deterrents to successful relationships. (You will also find more about self-love in Chapter 3). *Love yourself in order to be able to love others.* The adage is as old as the world. So of course when we begin our relationship life more or less in our late teens, if we've not learned to love the self, most of our relationships will - at the very least - face great hurdles. Especially when you add to that the fact that our partner will most likely *also* not have learned how to love the self. Two babes in the woods, so to speak, surrounded by a pack of snarling wolves in the guise of the ideas with which our culture imbues us. And it seems to be our best-kept secret. Oh, I know, most people *know* how important it is to love the self, but they are not necessarily aware of how greatly the lack of self-love impacts negatively on their relationships (as well as every other sector of their lives), and further, they have very little idea about how to go about learning to love the self. So nothing changes. Or they look for a new partner, hoping against hope that the pattern won't emerge again, and that they won't have to learn how to do that which they are uneducated about: loving the self.

The Shadow and Its Projection

Most of us are unaware of the *shadow,* an unconscious part of the psyche which has not been experienced and lived out. Jung believed that the more people truly know themselves by looking into themselves, the more society as a whole becomes conscious.

Children are often taught not to show - or even *feel* - their objectionable and aggressive urges. Although it's evident that they must be encouraged not to act out these urges, as opposed to understanding to recognize their appearance and then learning how to channel them in healthy ways, they may wind up repressing all conscious knowledge of these negative aspects *until they are buried so deep that they manage to forget their existence*. Thus, they believe that their chosen conscious attitude is who they really are. Jungian analyst and humanistic astrologer Liz Greene who has written many excellent books involving elements of the shadow, said of it: *You see the issue of the Shadow isn't a question of admitting faults. It's a question of being shaken right down to your foundations by realizing that you are not as you appear - not to others, but also to yourself.*

Clearly the negative aspects that get *buried* have not disappeared – they have simply moved into the unconscious (the cave, in Campbell's words) where they can cause all kinds of trouble when the shadow forces its way into outer behavior. You might, for example, inadvertently say the opposite of what you meant to say. Or behave in an unexpectedly outrageous, impolite, silly, or simply totally out-of-character manner. Often, unrecognized aspects of the self are what you notice - that which impacts you as something negative in other people: these are *projections*. You literally project out on to another individual something that lies within you because you are not yet aware of it in yourself. You are able to see it in the other, but not in yourself. So if you notice that a certain person (that you don't particularly like; perhaps even *dislike*) is very arrogant, or very tight-fisted, or very self-righteous, or very bigoted, or very uncompromising, or very exigent, or very impatient, or very judgmental, or very critical, then in all likelihood you are in fact, facing a facet of your own character that you have not, as yet, recognized.

> *Depth psychology has presented us with the undeniable wisdom that the enemy is constructed from denied aspects of the self. Therefore, the radical commandment "Love your enemy as yourself" points the way toward both self-knowledge and peace. We do, in fact, love or hate our enemies to the same degree that we love or hate ourselves. In the image of the enemy, we will find the mirror in which we may see our own face most clearly.*
> Sam Keen

The best clue to the existence of shadow aspects of the personality is the level of *affect* or emotion you have about another person's behavior. Does it bother you? Does it annoy you? Anger you? Enrage you? Until the content of the projection becomes conscious, projections continue to occur in a compulsive manner accompanied by intense emotion. But of course as long as it is a projection, you feel that the problem lies with the other person, never realizing that precisely because of your strong emotional reaction to the other person, the problem – or issue to be resolved – lies with you (whether or not the other person's behavior is acceptable is immaterial to this - that individual simply serves as a *tool*, a gem, in your own self-recognition and growth). The beautiful aspect of all of this is that the moment you become aware of the brilliance of this way of understanding your reactions to others, is the moment you can begin to free yourself of the shadow. Or better said: you can begin to incorporate the shadow into your life in such a way that it comes into the light, where you are aware of it, thereby *allowing you to let go of the need to project it on to others*. You will notice bit by bit as you do this that those who used to annoy or bother you, or cause some kind of negative emotional reaction in you, no longer do so. Perhaps a whole *new* projection will arise, allowing you to explore further aspects of your shadow, but the old parts will no longer rear their undeniably ugly heads and you will have freed a portion of your psyche from those restrictive manacles.

Jung felt that everyone has a psychological counter-sexual reality represented by the opposite sex. The *anima* (Latin term for soul or spirit), the feminine figure in a man's psyche, represents unconscious qualities in him. The flesh and blood women in his real life are a highly valuable source of information for a man about those things for which he has no eyes, or which simply have not yet come into his consciousness.

The *animus* is the masculine figure in a woman's psyche, symbolizing new creativity or potential within, as well as − on the negative side - rigidity, obstinacy, absolute convictions, or a sense of personal worthlessness. The flesh and blood men in her real life are - just as in the case of men in the paragraph above - a rich and valuable source of information for her about those things she is not yet aware of in herself.

We are *always* attracted to an outer man or woman who in some evocative fashion embodies *not yet lived out or realized* (and therefore projected) aspects of our own anima or animus. Dreams frequently provide richly symbolic material for exploring these aspects of the psyche and you can find some suggestions further explaining this in my blogs. In this instance, contrary to our discussion of the shadow above, the projection is very positive. That is why we fall in love with it. We actually fall in love with ourselves via the projection, i.e., with nascent bits of ourselves we have not yet seen, and so *we feel we need the other person because he/she is able to express what we cannot;* he/she embodies characteristics and traits that we *love* and that we believe we are not able to live without.

To understand *another* way projections occur, imagine meeting someone who is so amazing that for some reason when you are with that person, you feel loved by that person and hence feel you are loveable and are able to feel *love for yourself* in a way you have never before done. *It feels so immensely wonderful to love the self if this is not something you know how to do on your own.* And so if the presence of that other person in your life is what allows you to feel so good about yourself, obviously you want that person there for you (even though you are in all likelihood unaware of those psycho-emotional underpinnings to that 'good feeling'). And to make the whole thing even more complicated, since you may not know about projections and hidden aspects of the psyche, the fact that you feel so good when you are with that person, causes you to believe you love him/her. And of course, what is also happening is that you therefore *need* that person. And so the die is cast.

Since all of this is unconscious, it generally takes a falling away of the rosy glasses and a return to reality to force us into pain and frustration, making us begin the process of self-awareness, understanding, and thereby the process of growth towards the *incorporation of these needs and then to first fulfill them ourselves for ourselves, and to move towards a degree of wholeness from whence we can approach relationships very differently, and with a far greater measure of inner freedom.*

Apart from needing the partner because they love us - especially at the beginning during the honeymoon phase, and hence how *good* that makes us feel about ourselves - there are many other reasons we may need them if, as said, they are expressing characteristics that are also in us but that we have not yet brought forth. For example, a woman may fall in love with the inner strength, sense of justice or proactive behavior of her partner. Whether or not *he really is like that* is not the point, because if she has not yet *realized* those aspects of her own self, then the relationship will make her feel she needs the other (not knowing it is for these reasons) because *it brings her closer to her own real self, the self that she is not yet acquainted with.* Likewise, a man may fall in love with the sweet-tempered nature of a woman, her generosity, her ease in situations of emotional openness, her willingness to be vulnerable. Whether or not *she really is like that* is not the point, because if he has not yet *realized* those aspects of his own self, then the relationship will make him feel he needs the other (not knowing it is for these reasons) because *it brings him closer to his own real self, the self that he is not yet acquainted with.*

This altogether different slant of a relationship brings us to many new considerations. Perhaps the most important of these is the fact that once we know this and once we decide to live as if it all were true, because we desire with all our hearts to find the self and become intensely familiar with the self that heretofore has been an unknown element of ourselves, then we will do everything it takes to get to that place. And that means that we will undertake the task of beginning to love the self, and of looking on our relationships as instruments of transformation.

Relationships can bring great happiness, but that is not their purpose. You might call it an added benefit. The true and more primordial purpose of relationships is their transformative quality, if we will only allow it to happen. A relationship always offers the potential of serving as a mirror into the self. What this really means is that you start realizing that what is important for the well-being of your relationship is exactly the same thing as what is needed for your own spiritual growth. Each partner holds the pieces that the other is missing. If you are angry, suspicious, or jealous, for example, then these feelings bring up something in your partner that needs to be healed, and it is precisely that which is being mirrored in you. So you begin to see the importance of your partner's interaction with you for your development (and vice versa). So transformation or spiritual growth mean that the common denominator of the relationship becomes the idea that both partners are in the relationship to grow (and love, and trust, and be happy, and have great sex, and enjoy, etc., but with a continuous eye towards growth).

When you feel attracted to someone, it is because that person carries within them something that lights up your buttons *because there is something there that is unresolved in you.* It doesn't have to be a difficult or negative thing, simply something that has not yet been recognized or addressed, and the fact that you are now attracted to this specific individual, should be reason enough for you to realize that beyond the chemistry, beyond the infatuation, beyond the possible love, there is something even more important that can help you become more psychologically and emotionally free and whole, *and precisely this person can be the means - the tao - by which you get there*, as long as you realize the mechanism of the dynamics behind what is happening. In other words, don't go there without bringing yourself back to awareness, don't go into the relationship blindly. Look at yourself.

Understand that the attraction is a sign for you, a clue, a map, a *treasure* map, so that you will sit up and take notice. Your feelings are – in this sense – your road to freedom. Pay attention to them *beyond the obvious.* Learn to use them. Use them to grow. Grow and transform your way into freedom, because that is your duty to yourself and that is your right.

Keys For Understanding and Improving Your Relationships: A Plan to Follow

- Realize that attraction, love, chemistry, and emotion, come about due to the psycho-emotional and spiritual makeup of your inner man or woman precisely in order that you may work on these to further develop yourself. It is your psyche's way of helping to make you whole. That is why relationships are of such enormous importance in personal growth and development.
- Always watch any kind of "affect" (emotion, both negative and positive), as it gives strong clues about where you might be advised to work on something (even if it proves the other person is less than wonderful). But if you were "whole", your affect would not get involved because you would either have resolved the issue by communicating with transparency and awareness with the other person, continually bringing yourself back to that inner balance, or - if the person is indeed undesirable, you might have taken the decision to move on.
- Analyze arguments, NOT from the point of view of how egotistical, horrible, jealous, or domineering, etc. your partner is, but from the point of view of what the argument is telling you about YOURSELF. The other may indeed be all

those negative things, but it is much less important to dwell on his or her failings than on your own possibility for growth by observing your reactions to whatever is occurring.

- Use that knowledge to change, grow, and learn that you always have a choice in your reaction to any situation.
- Become very aware of yourself at ALL times - watch the times you would like to prevaricate, or at least, tell things in a way that is not 100% the real way, and try to discover why - are you afraid you will not be accepted or loved if you show your real self?
- Particularly watch those relationships that have an imbalance of power - if you are top dog - ask yourself what you get out of it, if you are on the bottom - why you are willing to be there. The answer to all of this serves your growth. Remember, it takes two to tango.
- Develop a sense of self by filling your own needs rather than by trying to fill them through others. *Love yourself first.* Remember that this has nothing to do with selfishness, and everything to do with creating and developing a healthy self.
- Observe and analyze yourself in a love relationship (and not just necessarily your current one) on the basis of this chapter.

Chapter 3

Required Thinking

I magine you learned how to drive a car with an automatic shift. You've done so for years. Now, however, you have acquired a car with a gear shift. The change is not terribly hard, *but it has to be learned.* Having a spiritual partnership, or wishing to grow into one, also has to be learned. If you don't change the way you think about relationships, this book will not help you and although this chapter overlaps with many of the concepts I wrote about in *Rewiring the Soul*, they need to be stated unequivocally for those who have not read that book, and even for those who have, but who haven't yet incorporated those ideas into their way of life.

Practicing the Art of Being Conscious

We are neither born conscious, nor are we socialized into being conscious. Rather - at least initially - we become a bit like sheep (yes, yes, me too). Most of us conform to peer pressure and to precepts established by our culture, at least for a while. And so we are asleep. And if we don't wake up, we haven't a shred of hope of establishing the kind of relationship I'm discussing in this book.

But let's say you are already on that road. Maybe that's precisely the reason why you picked up this book. You caught a glimpse of what could be - the way all of us do as we begin to awaken. And you want more of it. So now what? How does it happen?

Being conscious and remaining conscious require practice. How did Nadal, Federer, or Djokovic rise to be the number one player in tennis? How does a beginning golfer become good? How did Picasso create his paintings? You know the answer, of course. It was practice, and practice and more practice. Some discipline. And it was a firm belief in the value of what was being done and motivation to continue doing it - over and over and over again. Here's another way of looking at it: when you have a chipped tooth or a sharp edge on a molar, you know that your tongue goes there incessantly until eventually a very sore spot develops on it. It hurts. You wince each time your tongue goes there again in its unbidden and automatic way. So you *start becoming conscious* of your action. You stop your tongue halfway to the tooth. You *remember* not to do it because you now have a *vested* interest in not doing it. And so eventually what had become an automatic habit stops.

Becoming aware of the need to become conscious and then to remain conscious as much as possible all day long each and every day, is similar. Practice, discipline, intention, remembering to do it (or setting up reminders for yourself throughout your day, your house, your car, your office), and having a vested interest in the outcome of no longer succumbing to your automatic and blind ways of being, all form part of the road to awareness.

What are a few examples of being blind, especially in the relationship arena?

- Your partner says something hurtful. You place the blame for how you now feel on his/her shoulders. Being conscious would mean that you would take responsibility for how you feel *despite* the hurtful words. By not realizing (being conscious of) that your inner state of well-being is in your hands, you are fettered to reacting to whatever others do blindly and reactively and so you are not free.

- Your partner is despondent about a bad day at work. You also become despondent, or at least your mood turns slightly grey, in sympathy to his/her dilemma. Being conscious would mean that you would continue to remain balanced within your own being, potentially thus being able to offer better support and motivation to your partner. By not realizing (being conscious of) that the direction of your mood always needs to remain in your own hands, you will commit the error of mistaking sympathetic commiseration for compassion and so you are not free.

- You and your partner have been invited to a party. Your partner is flirting with another person of your own sex. A good-looking person, quite a bit younger than you. You get jealous. This is, of course - in your eyes - your partner's fault. Being conscious would mean that you would immediately recognize two possible scenarios: one - your partner has a habit of flagrantly flirting, you've discussed it in the past and asked him/her to stop it, so this is a clear transgression of a very important boundary, in which case there are several possible outcomes depending on how you decide to react (and you might also like to have a look at the topic of boundaries in the next section as well as in Chapter 6); two - your partner does not tend to flirt, you may be over-reacting, but above all, by being conscious you would recognize that your reaction of becoming jealous under these circumstances, says much more *about you*, than it does about him/her. Therefore, if you were aware, you would begin to look at the part of yourself that takes you down this nefarious road. In a conscious, spiritual partnership, obviously this would furthermore be discussed in a very transparent, loving, and non-judgmental way by the two partners.

Agreeing to Be Responsible for the Self

The fact that the title of this section contains the word 'agreeing' is quite deliberate. If you don't agree to do this, it simply won't happen. Agreeing means that you will put your every intention behind the desire and push to become responsible for the self. You will attempt to continually *be conscious* of it. And of course being responsible for the self means accepting responsibility for everything you think, feel, say, do, and how you react in the face of the behavior of others or any other outer circumstance in your life and in the world at large.

As long as you do not take on such a responsibility, you will continue to blame others and outer circumstances for how you feel and what you do and how you react. *I can't help it*, you may say; or *I've been dealt a bad hand;* or *I just can't trust anyone after having been treated that way.*

There is a bit of the victim in not taking on this responsibility for the self, or a bit of hanging on to our wounds and our pain, because of course as long as we can blame another or a circumstance for something in our lives, *no one* will expect *us* to do something about it. And so we can remain in our comfort zone. But not only does that mean that we would stagnate, it also means we would not be able to have a growth relationship: a spiritual partnership.

If my partner upsets me in any way, I first have to ask myself the question *is any of this mirroring something about myself back to me?*

If my partner is abusive (emotionally, psychologically, or verbally - I am not including physical abuse here as that is a topic of its own), obviously that is *not* my responsibility, but it is *very much* my responsibility what I then decide to undertake with regards to his/her abusive behavior, i.e., discussing it, going into therapy, making the decision to remove myself from the situation, or perhaps even reporting it to the police. But apart from all of the above, if I intend to be *consciously responsible* I need to try to understand how I entered into a relationship with an abusive person; what parts of me subconsciously responded to something in this individual when we met, because *clearly* something did, *even though at that point it was not evident that he/she was an abusive person*, although there generally tend to be clues of some kind that can be recognized retrospectively. You will recall what we discussed about patterns in relationships being a repetition of something that happened in childhood, *in order to finally put a problem to bed,* i.e., to resolve it on the level of the psyche and the spirit. Something in you *resonated* with feelings from your childhood (although at the time you may not recognize it as such) when you fell in love and this is the connection between you, the pattern, and your partner.

If my partner continually crosses boundaries, again, obviously that is *not* my responsibility but it is *very much* my responsibility what I then decide to undertake with regards to his/her boundary transgression. I will need to consciously recognize how much I *allowed* it, and which part of me needed for it to be allowed, i.e. what needs were getting fulfilled by permitting this boundary transgression. Did it allow me to see myself as a victim? Did it allow me to feel needed? Did it allow me to feel magnanimous (even while feeling resentful)? The topic of boundaries is vast, which is why I address it at some length in *Rewiring the Soul* and suggest you take another look there if they are not clear to you, as well as in Chapter 6 of this book. Boundaries are strongly linked to issues related to poor self-love and hence neglecting to resolve our own unhealthy boundary problems will negatively impinge on any positive results we are seeking with regards to our relationships. It is not easy to emerge from the depths of lifelong poor boundaries, but they must be faced and surmounted if we wish to live a vibrant and rich life filled with the possibility of inner well-being. Our primary relationships - our spiritual partnerships - can serve as the crucible in which we can learn to do this.

If I notice that due to an interaction of any kind with my partner I feel a negative emotion (anger, fear, jealousy, pain, despondency, etc.), it is *very much* my responsibility how I deal with my own feelings. First and foremost, long before I look at my partner, and see what needs to be changed there, I need to look at myself. What is it *in me* that has caused me to lose my inner balance? It is *my* responsibility to regain (or find for the first time) that inner balance, *no matter* whether my partner cleans up his/her act or not. Clearly I'm not saying that your partner should be absolved of responsibility, but it's his or her choice to take on responsibility *just as you are doing* and it is not *your* responsibility to try to change the other.

Furthermore, it is also possible that your partner has not, in fact, done anything at all, but that you nevertheless have had a negative reaction. Especially in such an instance, you need to be particularly careful in unraveling what is going on, if you want to live a conscious relationship. It is far too easy to blame another for your own negative feelings and that is why, the moment blame enters the picture, you need to be highly aware of what might be going on in you *in relationship to your partner,* much more, in fact, than what your partner just said or did. Clients often admit reacting negatively as far as their feelings are concerned, merely on the basis of a change in expression on the partner's face, or perhaps a small sound made by the partner. And while it is true that sometimes facial expressions and sounds express covert criticism, disapproval, and so on, it is also true that if that is the way it is being interpreted plus reacted to, then you are allowing yourself to be manipulated on the basis of your beliefs or thoughts. Conversely, you could react consciously on the basis of an aware choice you make after something has been said or occurred, after having some inner dialogue about it, and after having sought to regain a measure of inner peace and balance (all of which can happen in seconds, as you gain practice in using this *muscle*), which again brings us full circle to the need to being fully responsible for the self.

Admitting Choice At Every Turn

People are sometimes amazed at the freedom the mere acceptance of this concept brings into their lives: knowing that there is *always* a choice, no matter the circumstances, because where choice is never lost is in one's own inner reaction to any event. Oh, at first they may balk at the idea, giving many instances in which - according to them - there are no choices but there truly are no such instances.

- If your picnic is spoiled by rain you can choose to think differently about it being spoiled and decide to have fun indoors.
- If you are not accepted at the college or job of your liking, you can consciously choose to think differently about the outcome based on new plans that may open another set of doors.

- If you lose your job you can choose to think in ways that are not negative, even if only based on the fact that the more positive you keep your outlook, the better energy you will emanate, and the greater your possibilities for finding another position become.
- If you are jailed for 28 years like Nelson Mandela, or forced into Auschwitz like Victor Frankl, you can choose how to react inside, *even if that choice is one of the hardest things you have ever done in your life.*
- If your legs are amputated below the knee like Aimée Mullins, or if you are thrown from your horse and become a quadriplegic like Christopher Reeve, you can choose how to react inside, *even if that choice is one of the hardest things you have ever done in your life.*

Therefore, based on these examples, you can at least consider the possibility of *always* having a choice, no matter what your outer (and inner) circumstances, but obviously to make such a consideration part of your life and part of your relationship, is not something that will happen just because as you are reading this you now agree with it. You will need to practice it each and every time you are confronted with difficult situations and in so doing, you will additionally be practicing remaining conscious and accepting full and complete responsibility for all you think, feel, say, and do. Without this kind of thinking and behaving, the priceless jewel of spiritual partnership will forever remain out of your grasp.

Learning to Love (and Soothe) the Self: Finding Heaven

As long as we do not love ourselves, we need to seek love *for* ourselves in others. As long as we seek love *for* ourselves in others, we get a glimpse of heaven. It's a heaven we could create ourselves, but until we become aware of the psychological and spiritual dynamic that is occurring, we have no inkling of this potential for heaven in our very own self. Therefore feeling so good when we see love *for* ourselves in others, and feeling so devastated when that love is withdrawn, should give us a major clue to what is really happening. But what we see out there in films, magazines, commercials, books and talk shows, not to mention the reality shows, simply feeds our erroneous conception of how love is meant to work.

Think of it like this: if I am hungry, but don't know how to supply food for myself, and you are offering delicious food, it makes sense that I get it from you. But what happens when you disappear, or offer your supply of food to another person instead of me, or simply say I can't have any more of your food? I'll starve to death. I'll suffer, unless I can quickly find another food supplier. Or - and this of course is the correct alternative - unless I learn how to supply food for myself. So now I no longer need you. (Note: this book is *not* about learning how not to need others, but about understanding that as long as you don't love the self, your need for others will lead you down many rocky paths.)

Let's take the analogy one step further. You supply me with meat and fish and I supply you with fruits and vegetables. Both are necessary for our survival, and if either is withdrawn or lost, the other will suffer. And again, if I learn how to hunt and fish in order to supply myself with meat and fish, I no longer need you, and if you learn how to start a garden in order to supply yourself with fruit and vegetables, you no longer need me. But here's the thing: what if we meet when we already know how to do all of this and we begin a relationship based not on each supplying the other with a necessary dietary ingredient, but based on simply loving and enjoying each other's company?

Do you see how this changes the parameters of the relationship? Or what if one or both of us begins the process of figuring out how to get our own supply of the required food when our relationship has already been on-going for some time, and hence we stop needing it from our partner? That too, will change the parameters of the relationship. It might mean that our food supply partner decides they also want to learn how to get their own supply, or it might mean they want things to go back to the old *I need you - you need me* status quo. Either way, the relationship is no longer the same.

And that is basically how it works if at least one of the two in a relationship begins to become conscious and begins to take responsibility for making the choice of loving the self *at all times*. Now that you supply that so very necessary ingredient for yourself, you no longer need your partner in that very dependent way, and so you have the beginning of a relationship - approaching a spiritual partnership, based on complementarity rather than on need; on freedom rather than on chains, and on independence rather than dependence.

The significance of this is that you make a priority of this love for the self in ways that we don't typically consider, mainly because - as stated earlier - we are not raised this way by our families, nor are we socialized this way by our environment. You may take your own inner energetic reading (*how do I feel?*) first thing when you wake up in the morning in order to gauge what you may need to do in order to bring yourself to a place of inner balance. You do this *because you love yourself and consider this kind of taking care of yourself as part of your daily routine,* just as you would brush your teeth. You take this very seriously because you know that if you don't, you will not be fulfilling your own needs and your relationship may soon disintegrate into blindness again: a state of not being aware. You may need to do this throughout the course of your day on numerous occasions when life gets in the way and threatens to throw you off-course, and so you need to adjust your inner settings. You do this *because you love yourself and consider this kind of taking care of yourself as part of your daily routine,* just as you would check your temperature if you are developing a fever, and then, if necessary, take aspirin or go to see the doctor.

Also, clearly, loving yourself and making a priority of your inner state of well-being, and having made the decision that you wish to live a conscious spiritual partnership, means that when issues arise with your partner that threaten to make you feel pain or anger or anything negative at all, you will first and foremost - as part of this love for yourself - ensure that you bring yourself into a state of inner balance *before reacting* to whatever just happened.

The things you may do in order to correct your inner state, your negative emotions and your inner balance because of this love for yourself could be likened to what a loving parent does for a child that has hurt itself and comes crying for comfort, except that in this case you are your own loving parent. We learn to mother and father ourselves in ways that perhaps never happened when we were children. If they had, this whole process might just be a bit easier on us. But however it was then, what you can do now is not so difficult to learn. You may do a mindfulness exercise, a gratitude exercise and you may learn how to correct your self-talk (for all these exercises, see the Appendix. You may also work on maintaining your inner state of energy high). Above all, you will begin to treat yourself as the beloved that you are, learning to forgive yourself, learning to soothe yourself in healthy ways, being kind to yourself, and continually seeking inner balance and inner well-being.

Making a Daily Conscious Practice of Living Now

Not living in the present moment is tantamount to giving your life away. You know how it goes: if you are in your past or your future in your thoughts and/or emotions, you are not present, and hence you lose that present moment to the past which already happened, or to the future which has not happened yet. Either way, your present moment has been wasted. String a number of those present wasted moments together over the course of a day - perhaps one hour, and that is probably a very low estimate, and add that up over the course of a week, and you have seven hours. That would make 7 x 52 in one year which equals 364 hours. Divide that into 16 hour days (the time people are typically awake, assuming they sleep for eight hours), and you have about 23 days or *three whole weeks* per year that you are not living your life; that you are wasting your hours, and that you are literally throwing your life away. Imagine if you increase that daily number to one and one half hours, instead of only one. That would make 10.5 hours per week which comes to 546 hours per year, or 34 sixteen-hour days of lost time, lost *life* time. That's more than one entire month! Over a 75 year life span, and assuming you started doing this at age 10, that's the equivalent of about five and a half YEARS of your life spent not being present, not living your life. And I am confident that my assumption that most people spend far more than just 1.5 hours per day not being present will not be considered overly pessimistic.

In fact, recent (2012) research by psychologists Matthew Killingsworth and Daniel Gilbert of Harvard demonstrates that individuals may spend well over 40% of their time during waking hours having thoughts that are unrelated to what they are doing and this "mind-wandering" tends to make them unhappy.

Hopefully I've convinced you that living the present moment is very important. Perhaps you also understand that continually revisiting past pain or suffering, or frequently going into worry mode about potential future stress, problems and difficulty rarely, if ever, resolves anything. If you were given a poor health diagnosis, worrying about potential future outcomes will not improve your health. However, proactively seeking a solution, proactively undertaking changes in how you live your life might improve it, and neither of those two choices involves worrying and being stressed. On the contrary, they may not only improve your health, but they will concurrently move you into an enhanced energetic direction. You will *feel* better psychologically and emotionally because you are being proactive about the situation.

Likewise, *worrying* about financial problems, relationship difficulties, professional or social issues and so on, leads to little or nothing. Brainstorming, however, being proactive, getting another opinion, networking, etc., all can be useful in ways that worrying *never is*. What worrying does, however, is to take us away from our present moments and catapult us into the future when something bad *might* happen, or into the past when something bad *did* happen. As Wayne Dyer so famously said *if worrying were of any use, I'd be teaching seminars to show you how to worry better*. And Mark Twain said: *I've had thousands of problems in my life, most of which never actually happened.*

How this relates to spiritual partnerships, and why it is *required thinking* for living a spiritual partnership, forming part of the subtle melody of background music that this book is discussing, can best be explained by use of some examples:

- Continually harping back to the past: typically this happens because the partner who does it has not worked on resolving the past within him or herself. In part that may be related to boundary issues because if certain objectionable patterns of behavior are repeated over and over on the part of the other (shouting at you, habitual tardiness, lying, cheating, emotional unavailability), and they have been discussed but nothing changes, then the partner who keeps harping back on these issues *first* will need to work on his/her own boundaries in order to clear them and thus reach a point where he/she is capable of setting up consequences should the behavior in question be repeated, *and then stick to those consequences*. Once that is done, in theory, there will be no need to harp back on past issues. In other words, not living in the present damages not only you, but also the relationship. Not living in the present is not something an individual who is living a spiritual partnership would do, or, if he did, he would become aware of it, and begin to work on changing it.

- Continually worrying about the future - of the relationship, or your health, or your partner's health, or your mutual finances, or your children, or your parents, or the mortgage, or the family car, or the dog, or the kid's college education, or the state of your aging process and your partner's roving eye. You get the point. In other words, not living in the present damages not only you, but also the relationship. Not living in the present is not something an individual who is living a spiritual partnership would do, or, if he did, he would become aware of it, and begin to work on changing it.

- Continually - and this is a very common problem in 'normal' or conventional, traditional (as opposed to spiritual) partnerships - rehashing words in your mind that were said - to you or by you with regards to something that occurred with your partner. Perhaps you had a fight. Perhaps your partner left the house in a huff. Perhaps you did. Whatever happened, you are now going over and over and over those words that were exchanged, or events that occurred, or actions that were taken, trying to extract greater meaning from them, trying to figure out if you should have said or done something differently in order to prevent the outcome that resulted. Additionally, you may give a word-by-word replay to a close friend (or more than just one) and hence perpetuate your thinking about it even further. You can see clearly that such rehashing of a conversation or series of events is also another way of not living in the present, and furthermore, it rarely proves to be effective. The pro-active thing would be to look at your part of the conversation or event and attempt to understand what prompted you to say or do what you did, and the 'what' should not be something that you are blaming on your partner, *even if your partner did something reprehensible.* This is much more about you understanding your own issues with regard to the situation that just occurred, and what you might need to change. It's *not* about what your partner needs to change. That is his/her own responsibility. In other words, not living in the present damages not only you, but also the relationship. Not living in the present is not something an individual who is living a spiritual partnership would do, or, if he did, he would become aware of it, and begin to consciously work on changing it.

Living a Life With Purpose

Life with no intrinsic meaning or purpose, life without a significance that means something to *you* and that allows you to wake up in the morning, knowing that you have another opportunity today to make a difference, is something without which it is very difficult to live an independent, self-loving and conscious life. By purpose I'm not referring to having a mission to save the world, but I *am* referring to living your life in such a way that this purpose allows you to make a difference - on some scale. Whether you work for an NGO in sub-Saharan Africa, or volunteer to coach basketball every year with inner city youth; whether you paint glorious landscapes for others to feast their eyes on, or own a bakery where every product that you sell is a feast for the palate; whether you teach math to eight-year-olds in a small town in such a way that even those with little inclination in the numbers department, will have learned to forever love math, or whether you have elected to take on the drama club at your neighbourhood high school to show the participants what theatre is truly all about; whether you start a campaign to beautify forlorn sections of your community, or whether you run for office, all of it is important, and all of it gives you purpose.

Finding your purpose is another matter, and I spent some time discussing this in *Rewiring the Soul*, but suffice it to say, that with some connection to the self, and to the language of one's own body, finding a purpose and meaning for one's life is not impossible. But you *must* resonate with the thing that you decide to do; you must find some facet of it exciting, and because of that, we know that it is on a wavelength that actively resonates with your soul. Rumi said: *When you do things from your soul, you feel a river moving in you, a joy.*

Intending to Forgive

By forgiving we begin the process of severing our energetic connection to our past pain, trauma, abuse and hurtful memories of any kind. Without forgiving, it is extremely difficult, if not impossible to sever that connection, and that means that each time we think about the past pain or event, or each time it is somehow jogged back into our memory, we will not only suffer, but the strength of the pain can even increase, because we continue to give attention to it. Clients who endured a painful childhood, or relationship trauma due to deception or abandonment, or any other kind of hurt at all, and who tell me that they are unable to move beyond the pain, almost always also admit - once I ask the question - that they have not been able to forgive the party that injured them. They may often have tried, but with limited or no success whatsoever.

Understanding how to forgive most often lies at the crux of the matter. For most of us the idea of forgiving is somehow entangled with condoning what happened, and yet *nothing* could be further from the truth. By forgiving another for whatever way they have transgressed against us, we are healing ourselves. Ultimately, the act of forgiving is for the one who forgives. It is, one might say, a kind of agreement with the self, in which one chooses and decides to *intend* to forgive what was done, with the understanding that in so doing, the self will be able to move forward beyond the point of the pain and its memory. Each time the memory of the transgression or pain arises in your mind, think: *I intend to forgive, even if right now I don't yet know how.* In so doing, you weaken the neural pathways in your brain and the energetic connection to the pain, as opposed to strengthening them by continuing to think about whatever it was that happened. This simple and brief little exercise - consistently practiced - will eventually bring you to the place where you will *know* you have forgiven.

In *Rewiring the Soul* I used an example from the press: an American couple traveling in Italy with their young son, found him taken from them by a sniper's bullet. These grieving and bereft parents had many choices about how to react. Choices that anyone would have understood might have been anger, bitterness, and a desire for revenge. Instead, they chose to donate all the organs of their son's body to other families with children who needed them. In so doing, they were able to begin a process of forgiving and healing.

Many of us have seen instances in film and even on the evening news of a parent whose child (small or adult) was taken from them by a murderer, where the parent publicly announces - perhaps in court at the trial of the person who killed the child - that they forgive this murderer. *How*, we ask, *can they do this*? I believe, as do numerous other authors, that this is part of the process of healing. To forgive means to heal the self.

So far, all I've mentioned have been highly charged memories of difficult events. How does this apply to relationships? It's easy to understand how partners reach a point of so much past detritus of resentment for smaller or larger injuries, that the relationship becomes so bogged down, and one or the other is continually harping back to what the other did at some point this morning, yesterday, last week or five years ago, that there seems to be little possibility of salvaging the initial feelings of love.

And that is precisely where a conscious, loving, responsible and spiritual partner (or one who wishes to move in that direction) will realize that forgiving *must* be part of the plan. It is required thinking. Therefore when past problems surface, they must evidently first be addressed. If there are disloyalty issues, broken promises, shirking of responsibilities and so on, these *must* be addressed. The partner who feels the other is behaving improperly needs to discuss these matters with the other, but always from a self-aware point of view. As mentioned already, it is not a question of looking for someone to blame for any feelings of pain. First, I must take responsibility for my own feelings, but then I need to examine what I have done to share my feelings about the matter with my partner in an adult and mature fashion, i.e., not with anger or manipulation. Do I perhaps need to inspect my boundaries and how I handle them? Have my partner and I ever really discussed these matters, in ways that were not argumentative, but objective and rational? Have we ever - in the past - come up with a plan, a guideline of sorts to help us maneuver through the rocky waters of a growing relationship? (For more about this "guideline", see Chapter 6).

But once this has been tended, or once this road has at least been embarked upon, a next major step is to consciously forgive past transgressions my partner may have committed, *in order that I may* come to healing. It's about *my* healing. It's about the realization that from this point forward we are each responsible for our own thoughts, feelings, words, deeds and reactions, and that it is no longer kosher to blame the other, *even when their behavior leaves much to be desired.* This point is perhaps always one of the most difficult to grasp. How can I possibly not blame the other when their behavior has been so blatantly inconsiderate or unfair or outright cruel? You see, as we discussed earlier, it is never about *them.* It's always about *your* reaction to it or them. What you now decide to do or implement once this behavior has occurred, is very much *your* responsibility. How they continue to act or react is *theirs.* Somewhere in there, real and transparent communication between the two partners needs to have taken place as indicated above, but at some point one or both need to begin to consciously assume responsibility for the self, including being willing to *intend* to forgive.

A small note about what Eckhart Tolle calls the *pain body,* and Chris Griscom calls the *emotional body.* One of the principal reasons - according to these authors - that we continue going back to past pain *before* we recognize the need to forgive and *before* we begin to consciously *intend* to forgive is because of our great familiarity with the pain, the thoughts and the feelings that are connected, glued, we might say, and stuck to it. This great familiarity with pain makes us feel, when our thoughts go down the road they have traveled so often already, to the painful moment in our history, in some fashion that we are *at home*. Not in a loving or warm and comfortable home, because of course, it hurts immensely, but a home nevertheless because *we know it well*. We have been here so often that when our thoughts turn in this direction, we find it nearly impossible to withstand the pull, the nearly *seductive* urge to follow that route once more. And so we give in to that urge. We don't fight it. We go over the same sad material one more time. In so doing, of course, all neural pathways associated with that event and all its memories, become that much stronger by virtue of the continual reinforcement of those memories and thoughts. However, once conscious of this dynamic, we are now in a position to fight this. Each time our thoughts and feelings go down that well-trodden path again, we are now capable of beginning an inner dialogue of negation. An inner dialogue in which we firmly refuse to go down that road again. We may need to fight this battle several times before we actually achieve our goal, but once accomplished for that first time, it will become easier each time that follows. We will find ourselves feeling strangely elated, lighter, and empowered. And that process will begin to erode the neural pathway associated with the memory, and the pain body or emotional body that was erected around this particular theme, begins to crumble. The new habits in turn, will create another set of neural pathways capable of enhancing our inner well-being in totally novel ways, simply because we are no longer going down that same old path of disenfranchisement.

Clearly if both partners are not on the same wavelength, i.e., if only one of the partners has accepted the relationship as growth-oriented; as that which I am labeling a spiritual partnership in this book, then matters will not necessarily be easy. Possibly the partner who is not yet on that track, will observe the changes in the other with astonishment, and then notice an inner urge, a desire, to move in that direction as well. On other occasions, the partner who has not yet begun the *journey* towards spiritual partnership will insist on returning to the earlier status quo. What then ensues is very individual to each situation, but as you can imagine, in this latter case, the partner who has begun to grow, will find it exceedingly difficult to return to an earlier strait-jacket way of thinking and behaving, and hence this may be the breaking point in the relationship that then culminates in a separation or divorce.

Forgiving is as essential to a conscious partnership, as water is to plants. Choosing not to forgive, or believing that you do not have the capacity to forgive means that in some fashion you have not yet set yourself on the road to the different elements of required thinking as postulated in this chapter. Learning how to forgive is more a matter of intention, as stated, than a matter of knowing how to do it. Once the intention is set, you can begin. *Especially* if you recognize that it forms part of your growth process.

Chapter 4

Communication:
How It Generally Plays Out

The manner in which we communicate with our partner is frequently at the center of a failing relationship, or one that is on the road to failure. Perhaps we do not listen, either because we are already mentally preparing our reply, or because we hear something different than that which is being said by jumping to conclusions, or because we *believe* our partner means *this*, and therefore do not hear *that*. Perhaps we do not say what we really mean (we may not *know* what we really mean, or we may be afraid to say it for myriad reasons, most particularly because it might expose us in some way, leaving us vulnerable and open to pain, criticism, rejection, or ridicule, to name only a few), perhaps we fear *hearing* the truth, perhaps we are so filled with past pain and resentment that we are *unable* to hear the actual words being said.

It is also more than possible that we simply do not *know* how to communicate. Perhaps our mode is to be loud and insistent, even belligerent, or conversely, to pull down the shutters and batten the hatches when the going gets rough. Remaining silent, in some ways, is just as damaging as shouting. Not engaging is perhaps one of the most insidious and toxic aspects of a relationship for all concerned. Perhaps we come from a difficult home where our own parents communicated in ways that were not healthy and so we have carried this dysfunctionality over to our adult relationships where our partner may also not be well-versed in the art of healthy communication. Perhaps we never learned that under certain circumstances when one person says something, what is understood by the other may be diametrically opposed to the intended meaning. As you can imagine, such a situation causes enormous difficulties if the partners are not aware of this.

In the sections that follow and in very distilled fashion, I touch upon some major areas of contention in relationship communication that could all be improved immensely by the initial step of becoming conscious of yourself, then by taking on the responsibility for yourself already discussed earlier, and by continually observing yourself with total honesty in order to check for projection, blame, unhealthy boundaries, victimhood, and other apparently *easy* ways out of shouldering your part of the growth process in this silken web that makes up spiritual partnership and that promises such amazing brilliance of being.

The Blame Game

I most frequently encounter clients who come in for relationship issues telling me what their partner is doing wrong and that this behavior is the reason why they are unhappy or desperate or in pain and that is also the reason - according to them, why the relationship is failing. *If only my partner would ...* is perhaps the most common phrase I hear. And yet, as we have already seen, blaming the partner for *anything* at all, does not really resolve the problem.

But blaming the other is - evidently - the easiest way of glossing over your own responsibility in the matter. It's the easiest way of washing your hands of the matter as you cast responsibility for what is wrong with the partnership on the other.

Let me be totally clear: *however* your partner is behaving, or *whatever* your partner is saying, all of that is his or her *own* choice and own responsibility. But how you then *react* is totally your *own* responsibility. How are you reacting with a partner who manipulates you? How do you react when your partner lies? Cheats? Yells? Doesn't do his/her fair share of the chores? How do you react when your partner restricts what you can do? Tries to control your political or religious thinking? How do you react when your partner hacks into your email account or your mobile phone text messages? How do you react if your partner shows that spending time alone with you is not something he/she really wants to do? How do you react if your partner is an alcoholic or addicted to some other substance? How do you react if your partner criticizes even the smallest amount of money you spend? And how do you react to your feeling of being helpless and resentful in the sway of such criticism, if, perhaps you are not contributing to the household finances? And how do you react if your partner sides against you when the children want to do something that you have already vetoed?

If your reaction to all of this is that your partner is behaving out of line and that changes need to be made, implying that those changes need to be made by your partner, you are only partly correct. While it may be true that your partner has issues, or leaves a lot to be desired, the *real* question is: *have your reactions* to his/her behavior been the reactions of an individual who is fully conscious and prepared to accept responsibility for himself? Did you, for example, set up healthy boundaries, when your partner was trespassing yours? Do those boundaries come with consequences should they be ignored again? Many, if not all of the examples of poor partner behavior fall under the general umbrella of boundaries being crossed. What is yelling, if not the crossing of a boundary? What is lying, if not the crossing of a boundary? What is manipulation (emotional, financial, sexual, to name only a few), if not the crossing of a boundary?

It is, to restate the obvious, *your reaction* to all of this that exemplifies how conscious you are of yourself, and how willing you are to take on responsibility for yourself and *your inner well-being*. This is in diametrical opposition to blaming your partner. If your partner is not taking on responsibility for his or her own behavior, and if your partner is not willing to look at some of the concepts discussed here, then you *still* have a responsibility to yourself with regards to how *you* react to this unwillingness. In some ironic fashion - no matter what has happened (barring physical violence) - the buck stops with you!

Owning Your Feelings & Allowing Others to Own Theirs: Releasing Projection & Manipulation

The concept of owning your feelings is closely related to the foregoing section about blame. If *you make me feel* sad, angry, jealous, etc., these feelings in me are *your responsibility*, or, stated slightly differently, are your fault. However, if I *own* those feelings, and assume responsibility for them, then things begin to take on a very different shape indeed. Given the same behavior on your partner's part, if you become responsible for your feelings and own them in the same way we claim ownership for our belongings, then you perhaps begin to see that by owning them, you also can *choose* to be in *control* of them.

Choosing to be in control of your feelings; owning your feelings when your partner does this or that, literally means having a choice about how you feel, or, and this is perhaps a more easily understood first step - having a choice about what story (self-talk, self-dialogue) you now tell yourself about those feelings that have arisen in you due to your partner's actions or words. *Imagine the freedom!* I know the concept has not yet been properly explained, but just imagine the freedom such a choice would give you!

Let's summon a possible multi-layered scenario: you have just discovered that your partner has lied to you about something very important. You have had some conversations about lying in the past and you have set up boundaries about lying to you again, along with a consequence should it occur. If the lying is about small issues such as *'I took out the garbage'* when in reality I did not, the consequence would be very different from farther-reaching lies such as *'no, I did not sleep with that person'*. In the former case, you might have previously agreed that the consequence would be that there was a monetary fine such as five dollars, and it goes into my kitty for me to spend as I wish. In the case of the latter, and graver lie, the consequence might be (and you would have discussed this potential consequence previously) that if there were a reoccurrence of that grave lie then he/she would now need to move out of the house.

But let's address the issue of your feelings and owning them. In both cases you will feel disappointed, to say the least. In the latter case you will feel hurt, rejected, jealous or used and many other negative feelings of this type. How can you begin to *own* these feelings? What kind of *story* can you choose to tell yourself about this occurrence in order that you can regain some measure of inner peace and balance? What does a conscious individual do in such a situation?

First you breathe. Next you remember that you need to continue to remain conscious as opposed to reverting to your blind behaviors of another time in your life. Remaining conscious means that you will be able to tell yourself that you always have a choice about how you react in any situation of any kind, no matter what. Next, you may ask yourself if you could possibly stand away from your immediate strong emotions and just observe them; just breathe into them. What you are after in this process, is to find a way of reestablishing some level of inner balance before you continue and before you react in any way. *None of this is shoving the problem (your partner's lie) under the carpet.* All of this aims at allowing you to find that balance in order to be able to react in a way that *serves* you as opposed to reacting blindly and reactively which ultimately merely heaps greater ill-will and problems on an already over-burdened relationship.

This small role-play demonstrates the type of inner dialogue you could have in a moment of high emotion - *if you hold on to yourself* - and if you have been practicing some of the things we've been discussing in earlier chapters of this book. If you have not practiced any of it, you will find that a situation of this type may throw you for a loop because you have not developed any 'muscles' to help you in a moment of need. But if you have been practicing, and if you have managed to hold on to yourself by remaining conscious, does this mean your strong emotion will be gone? No. But it means you will have managed to view it through the lens of an inner relaxation or loosening of some of the tension - however slight. And that means you will not need to ride the roller coaster of inevitable blaming and pain and resentment that you normally would.

Your next question in this inner dialogue you are conducting with yourself would be to ask yourself if this situation serves any further purpose in your life. Perhaps it does. In that case, more transparent communication needs to take place between you and your partner. Or perhaps it is time to bring in the consequence of asking your partner to move out. And of course there can be many degrees of shading and variation between these two possibilities. But all of it arises from a conscious awareness of your feelings that you claim as your own and not from a position of blind reactivity and blame. Getting to the place where *you* decide how you will react in a given situation with high emotional content is a step toward spiritual partnership and inner freedom.

How do you allow your partner to own his or her own feelings? If your partner blames you for something he feels (as I have been attempting to encourage *you* not to do in the preceding paragraphs), then you need to refuse ownership thereof. He needs to assume responsibility for his feelings, no matter what you did. Obviously if your behavior is unkind, inconsiderate, abusive or cruel, you need to be looking at yourself under a very sharp lens indeed, but nevertheless, and despite that, it is still necessary that your partner take on responsibility for the feelings he has *allowed* to arise in himself due to your behavior. In other words - just as I am asking *you* to do, *he/she* also needs to consider becoming aware.

In a similar fashion, if your partner speaks of feelings that you do not understand, or find ludicrous or childish or anything at all, you must *allow him/her to own those feelings*. Just because they make little sense to you for a multitude of reasons you consider logical, you must first open yourself to the fact that as your partner expresses these feelings, they need to be allowed and respected. Once that is achieved, anything and everything can be discussed. But first allow them to breathe.

This assuming of responsibility for one's own feelings, claiming them as one's own, is a rather convoluted aspect to spiritual partnership and creates much confusion and difficulty for most of us at the beginning. Blaming the other is *so* much easier. But as long as we blame, we do not grow. And as long as we blame, we are not approaching spiritual partnership. This path to growth -

this *tao* - is not easy, but mainly because it seems so foreign, so different from our classic behavior in relationships to this point.

The Need to Be Right: Your Ego and My Ego

As long as you need to be right - for whatever reason - conscious and spiritual partnership will not be possible. Needing to be right is very much an ego matter. If you need to prove to another how right you are and how wrong he is, your ego is clamoring for attention, and you are failing to see the reality of what is going on. Clearly this is not a question about things that are easily checked, such as the capital of a country, or the metric equivalent of one yard. This pertains to opinions, ideas, ideologies, religions, philosophies, ways of living one's life, in other words, all those ephemeral, evanescent things that populate our lives, our thinking and feeling, and yet that have no *true* right or wrong.

If you give up your need to be right it is no longer possible to argue with you, you don't need to convince anyone of anything, and as an added benefit, you can keep yourself firmly in control with no problem whatsoever. More *importantly*, the other person begins to understand that you do not consider your opinion more worthy of consideration than his. That goes a long way to improving communication. Your ego is no longer invested in proving anything to the other person, so you feel great no matter what the other person decides to believe. This means there are no more power struggles because you give up the need to control others' behavior, thoughts, actions and reactions, and so, in conclusion, your life becomes a lot easier.

When you give up the need to be right - as said, in those areas where there is no clear right or wrong answer - you are opening the road to another kind of communication. You are, in effect, saying to the other person that you are willing and able to respect their opinion despite the fact that yours - about that particular matter - is very different. Eventually this makes for proactive and connected dialogue that is far more interesting than dialogue mired in conflict.

Evidently it's one thing to say this about something political, ideological, or philosophical, perhaps even religious, but quite another, if the topic of discussion is whether we should take out a second mortgage on the house, or whether the kids should go to public or private schools, or whether we should go into debt to buy a car for our eldest son. We might be arguing about the benefits of transferring to another city, about whether it's ok if I quit my well-paying job in order to subsist on your salary alone, so that I can go back to university, or whether our 16-year-old daughter should be allowed to date or stay out after midnight. All of these subjects are hampered by the fact that they have no clear-cut right or wrong answer.

In these cases, giving up the need to be right *does not* mean that you lie down on the floor and ask the other person to walk all over you, because what they want is what will happen. Rather, giving up the need to be right means that by not insisting that *your* opinion is the only right one, you're giving a very clear indication that you are allowing love to be the final determinant. You are showing that you want both sides to be on the table - equally - and that your desire is that clear and transparent communication about the matter take place between the two of you. And believe me, this works wonders with your teens as well. Perhaps not on the first try, but bit by bit things change when a teen recognizes that the parent is more interested in the love in the relationship - and in giving that love priority - than in being right.

It's also valuable if you can begin the process of looking at your relationship with the other person as an indicator about you, rather than an indicator about him or her. So instead of thinking *it's all his/her fault, and if only he/she would change, all would be well*, think instead, what can I do to change my way of dealing with this situation? Ask yourself how you can look at the difficulty from the point of view of *your attitude* in each problematic situation. This is *not* about *you* being wrong, but about you looking at the problem with an *out-of-the-box* attitude.

So when any of the things happen that tend to happen, and that make life so miserable, you could stand back, assess the situation instead of reacting to your buttons having been pushed, and begin to *choose how to react*, from a position of love and compassion, and from a place where you have decided *in advance* that you will not fight over who is right or wrong, but that you will do your utmost to promote understanding, trust, and love. And in all instances, please do remember that healthy boundaries are important, and that putting love first *never means you should let anyone walk all over you, or mistreat* you.

When you give up the need to be right you are not saying that what the other person believes is right, is also right for you. Whatever your opinion was continues to be your opinion. And you allow others to continue in their own belief.

Ask yourself this: *exactly why is it so important to convince the other person that you are right*? What will change? Because you do realize that if they feel just as you do, and believe that it is crucial to convince you of how right they are, you are at an impossible impasse, unless one of you is stronger than the other. If you are the parent, or the boss, or the one with the money, or the one who manipulates better, or the one who *needs* the other one less emotionally, then of course you will probably win.

Here's what will happen next: you will have growing resentment on your hands which will, eventually, explode. That's how revolutions and coup d'états come about, not to mention acrimonious divorces and bad relationships between parents and children. *Resentment from having to give in to a stronger party can be poisonous.*

What can you do if you are married to someone who wants to do things a given way and you do not? Do you get divorced? Do you give in? Or do you find a win-win solution where each party may need to give up part of what they believed in, in exchange for a solution that works for both? This latter possibility is only feasible if *both* parties are willing to give up the need to be right about *their* way of doing it, and agree that there could be a third way, one that gives *each* of the partners a degree of satisfaction. And by the way, *this is never 'not' possible.*

Here's another thing: once you give up the need to be right, you start listening to what others have to say - really listening, instead of impatiently waiting for them to stop talking, so that you can have your turn (to talk about all the things you are thinking about while they are talking). And not only do you start listening, you start to become interested in what they are saying *even if you don't think it's right*, because by giving up the need to be right, you begin to see others in a new light, a light of generosity, non-judgment and non-criticism. That space, where you can accept them as they are as opposed to wanting them to be *your* way, is a sacred space because it's one of the steps that leads you towards the understanding that we are all one and therein lies another kind of freedom, not only on the individual level, but also on the global one. And it is also a sacred space because it becomes a repository for connection on the deep inner level that forms part of spiritual partnership. (Note: portions of this last section are also found in *Rewiring the Soul* under the topic of the ego.)

Refusing to Engage & Mixed Messages

Many potential reasons exist for people to send mixed messages, as well as for refusing to engage, but all lead to the same result: poor communication, resentment and hurt, and the perception of coldness and deception. By refusing to engage, I need not claim *my own feelings*, as discussed in a previous section, because I can hide behind a mask of aloofness in the face of a needy or desperate partner, remaining in what appears to be - at first glance - the role of the objective partner, the one that does not give in to difficult and irrational emotions and scenes. What generally ensues is a more and more frantic partner, who at this point may indeed be quite beside himself, thus *proving* my point about his hysterical behavior. And in the meantime, I have not had to claim ownership of my emotions that probably arose and threatened to overwhelm me (which is why I used the defensive measure of refusing to engage, because it is how I learned to cope long ago), with regards to something my partner wishes to address.

Sending mixed messages is another way of avoidance by not assuming responsibility for a *clear* message, but which often implies either a firm commitment or the opposite, a resolute decision to break off a relationship. Therefore if I like a potential partner very much, and the reasonable thing to do would be to let her know, but instead I see her three days in a row and then don't even call, let alone see her for the next week or two, I am sending a mixed message (I like you, I like you not), but I am probably doing so because of my own fear of emotional vulnerability. In this way I manage to keep some control, and hence feel more secure, than if I had expressed my feelings for her clearly. (Note: to those who have already established healthy boundaries, this behavior would signify an immediate demand for transparency and clarity, and if refused, would most probably end the burgeoning relationship because of what such mixed messages and refusal to be transparent indicate about the potential partner). Nevertheless, the sad reality is that those who send mixed messages generally tend to attract people into their lives whose boundaries have not yet been cleared and hence the mixed message behavior may not be liked - may even be resented - but is generally tolerated and brings with it much potential heartbreak.

Another typical example of mixed messages goes in the opposite direction, although its outward manifestation is very similar to the one just described. If I know that a potential partner will never really be 'the one' for me, and that I am, in fact, not interested in building up a relationship with him or her, but either for reasons of pity or guilt, or conversely, for reasons of fear of not having enough eggs in my own basket, I now see this person often enough for him/her to believe there is hope, and yet - while never spelling out the truth - in so many other ways, I show this person that I am not truly available.

Acknowledging (at the very least to myself) that I either refuse to engage or send mixed messages or that I do both is a required step if I am going to attempt having a growth-oriented and spiritual partnership. In order to acknowledge such behavior, I must first become conscious of it. Once that has become clear to me, I must then accept responsibility for this type of behavior and then assume further responsibility for clearing the issues that have caused this defense mechanism to spring up in my life. It is possible to do all of this within the confines of an existing relationship, as long as complete transparency (see the section that deals with this topic further in this chapter) is practiced by both partners.

Boundaries

In order for boundaries to be upheld and respected by both parties, each needs to have become at least slightly conscious. As long as you don't understand that when you allow your partner to trespass your boundaries you are continually showing yourself that you do not love yourself, you will look at boundary violation by your partner as an act of unkindness, as inconsiderate behavior, and so on. In other words, you will blame what is *out there*, as opposed to taking on responsibility for caring for yourself and then beginning to set up the healthy boundaries.

Because so much about boundaries has already been discussed, both in this book, as well as in *Rewiring the Soul*, suffice it to say that the upholding of boundaries, the understanding and recognition that consequences *must* form part of this issue, and that in the conscious and self-respecting way of practicing how to uphold both boundaries and consequences, you take one of the most formidable steps in growth-oriented spiritual partnership, as well as in loving yourself. This step alone has the potential to move you much further and much more quickly than any other. (In Chapter 10 you will find one path towards beginning to set up healthier boundaries.)

Insistence on Being Blind: Not Taking Responsibility for the Self

It's so much easier to remain blind and asleep, isn't it? Like a baby in the womb, or in the cradle being rocked to sleep. No responsibility.

Life as a small child was great - I always found someone or something to blame for whatever was going wrong. My older brother wouldn't let me come along to play with his friends, the girl down the street had broken my favorite doll *on purpose*, the weather had spoiled our long-awaited picnic, my mother had scolded me harshly, I would tearfully tell my father when he returned at night, the 'bad' lady at the park made me get off the swing so others could use it, the 'nasty' friend had not let me win the board game. As you can imagine, I had a lot to learn.

And learn I did! But in that learning, and in the realizing that the more you take on full responsibility not only for all you *do,* but also full responsibility for all you think, feel, say, and above all, for *how you react* to those things that happen, meant that I began to see life with totally different eyes.

And of course, doing that means there is *no one left to blame.* No matter what happens, and no matter what another does.

That is ridiculous, you say:

- The government and the financial system which it allowed for so many years has wreaked havoc with our lives so much, that many of us are living on the brink of poverty. That is *clearly* the government's fault.
- Or: my car was totaled in that accident yesterday when someone ran the red light, and that is *clearly* the other driver's fault.
- Or: I've been diagnosed with breast cancer, and that is *clearly* the fault of my genes plus the environmental pollutants.
- Or: I've been training for national qualification as an equestrian jumper, but my father has been so negative about it all, stressing me every time I go practice, that I didn't make the grade, and that is *clearly* my father's fault.

We could come up with any number of other examples, but what I wanted to show by using these in particular, is that even in cases where many of us might agree that it is so obviously not *my* fault, if something of this nature occurs, I would still say: *but you must take full responsibility for how you react;* for how you *choose* to react.

> *Take your life in your own hands, and what happens?*
> *A terrible thing: no one to blame.*
> Erica Jong

Because of course much of this is a question of seeing that there is always a choice. A choice of how much attention I pay to what is happening in the government, first at my community and local level, then provincial or state, and so on, and finally at the federal level. I also have choices about the kind of car insurance I have and what it covers, and while I don't have a choice about the genes I inherit, I do have a choice about how I *influence* those genes on the basis of much of the information that is coming out of cellular and molecular biology (and it is *my* choice to read about these things so that I am informed), not to mention what I allow into my 'environment', which includes not only what I breathe, eat and drink, but also how I live, how I manage stress, with whom and what I am surrounded, and so on. And finally, I always have choices about how I react to others' negativity. I even have choices about how much time I spend with people who are negative - even a father.

But while I stand by the last paragraph, I believe that much more important even than that, is the choice to always assume responsibility for your own reactions. Find a place within where you gain equanimity and inner balance about whatever it is that is happening, and then, and only then, begin to decide what to do about it. Some things we can change. Others we can't change. But what we can *always* do, is to love the self so much, that our first priority is the recuperation of this inner balance. *That* is the first and the most gigantic step in not blaming another or a circumstance and in accepting responsibility for yourself.

Transparency

Who hasn't lied in a relationship? Maybe not about something as shattering as having an affair on the side, but perhaps something more light-weight such as pretending to like football or opera at the beginning so you can be with the football or opera lover, when in fact, it scarcely interests you. And who hasn't been lied to in a relationship – and felt the results: lack of trust and a general sense of malaise that permeates everything from that point forward, because you just don't know anymore whether the person that lied once can be trusted to not lie in future.

Transparency and the lack of it in relationships, is a condition with consequences whose insidious tentacles extend much further than pure and simple lying. Transparency means saying what is really inside of you. Transparency means not equivocating about what is important to you. It is not pushing your opinions or likes and dislikes on others, but it is being honest about them when they become part of what is happening in the relationship. Being transparent implies being vulnerable, because the transparency - the visibility of your inner self - is now out in the open, for your partner to see, to palpate, to react to, to comment on, and possibly, to reject. Clearly, this latter reason, coupled with the fear most people have of being vulnerable, causes many to avoid the issue of transparency. *If I allow him or her to see the real me, or so one reasons, he/she will not want to be with me, or will think I am too this or too that.* And yet, if you do not allow the other to see the real you, how will they ever truly know you? And therefore, if they fall in love with you, what or who are they falling in love with? It will be a chimera, evanescent by nature, since it is not real. Is it not better to risk possible rejection by being transparent, and thus eventually be loved for one's real self by someone who appreciates it, than to be loved for what one is not?

In some ways we could substitute *honesty* for transparency in the title of this section, but I believe that the latter term encompasses so much more than the former, while simultaneously containing honesty at its core.

Imagine a world without real conversations with those closest to us. Where would we be in such a world and how could we possibly uphold a relationship with a loved one without breaking through the barriers of conventional communication that keep us at a safe or polite distance from so many people in our own world? We need to know that our verbal, emotional, and physical contact - involving our psyche, emotions, and spirit - with those people in our lives that really matter to us is more important than many other things. If we are unable to connect at levels that delve deeply into ourselves, we are living at the surface of life and of the relationship with little hope of becoming profoundly intertwined.

Some people talk about energetic connections between individuals who are important to each other, connections between lovers, or between parents and children, and even connections between friends, and it certainly appears that these connections exist. Something traumatic may happen to one person in the relationship, and the other person, even though he may be thousands of miles away, knows something happened at exactly the same moment in time. Countless stories tell us about the veracity of this. What I am talking about here, however, is the connection that exists between two people who speak their truth to each other, and who connect - among other things - through their conversations. This can happen if you truly talk to the other person, and it can happen if you open yourself, not only to the other person, but to your own inner truth.

What does talking to another person have to do with your own inner truth? Quite a lot. If you aren't aware of yourself, if you aren't honest to yourself about yourself, it will be quite difficult to talk to the other person at the levels I am describing. Your conversations with others – even with important others – will not touch the rock bottom of your truth. And hence will not connect you to that person in a way that leads to true communication. So do talk. And *really* talk. But above all, become aware of yourself in order to be able to talk in the way this chapter recommends.

★★★★★★★★★★★★★★★★★★★

Clearly, as long as we continue to communicate with each other without knowing ourselves and without being aware, what we say, and what we understand when our partner speaks, and what our partner says and understands, will often be far removed from what was intended. And even if it is not, without inner clarity about all the points discussed in this chapter, our communication will often be fraught.

Changing this is not as difficult as it is to recognize that we need to do it. We may hit our head against the wall many times before we finally see the light, and that is precisely why and where relationships can play such a major role. Between the recognition of the need for change and the road we eventually walk to get there, is the place where we will encounter - at long last - the spiritual partnership we were meant to have.

Chapter 5

Vulnerability and the Willingness (Or Not) to Look at Yourself

We like to be in control. It means that the borders of our comfort zones remain intact and so there is no need to cross over into unknown territory. Being in control also means that no one carries more weight than we do in a given relationship. It may even mean that we are the one who calls the shots - in the arena of emotions and needs. Furthermore, it means we don't find ourselves being vulnerable, exposing ourselves to unfamiliar *and feared* emotions that we may have spent years avoiding or protecting ourselves against in prior relationships. Being in control offers a measure of security, it keeps us well within the safe confines of the known, the status quo, the comfort zone where no reaching and stretching is required. It is also the place where no growth occurs.

Getting Hurt

We learn quickly in life that love can hurt. Perhaps it's not even love, but we *think* it is. First with our parents, who may love us dearly, but hurt us nevertheless due to their own lack of awareness, maturity, and understanding about love, and occasionally the source of our pain lies with another kind of parents who *don't* love us and then hurt us emotionally or psychologically or physically and evidently such hurting leaves indelible marks.

But when we get hurt in our later love relationships, we begin to have different reactions. Who hasn't been through relationship pain? Who hasn't curled up into a ball (even if it's inside your head) with the pain that some element of a relationship has caused? Who hasn't wished that a portion of the life lived could be erased, could be forgotten, that by magic some form of amnesia would take over the brain, just to not remember whatever it is that is causing the pain? So what can be done? How do you deal with this?

Alcohol, recreational and prescription drugs, religion, praying, meditating, panic attacks, hyper-ventilating, spending large pockets of time on social networking sites, shopping, gambling, sex, frenzied social activity, numbness sought in movies, books, etc., are some of the self-soothing mechanisms people use to self-medicate in times of such deeply-felt relationship pain.

None of it really takes you anywhere. None of it is really of any lasting use. Oh, it may get you through the worst of your pain, but it doesn't really help you deal with whatever the underlying issue may have been. The problem is not so much that there is relationship pain that was apparently caused by the actions of another person, but that you are reacting with such intensity and such pain.

You see, when another person behaves in a way that hurts you, or does something that goes way beyond hurt, and that leaves a deep-seated mark on you in such a way that you feel that you will never be the same again, then there is something forgotten or buried inside of you - beyond the pain caused by the other - that needs attention. Basically what that means is that a good portion of your pain has to do with elements of yourself that have not yet been worked on by you, and that is why the actions of the other hurt so much. In other words, those same actions by the other would be perceived very differently by a person who has already begun the process of working on themselves. One of the things that needs looking at is your awareness of yourself and what it is that brought you to the place you are currently at. Another piece of the puzzle has to do with the choices you make at every step of the way: choices that you make when you act, react, feel, and think. Awareness - being fully conscious of yourself - and making choices are two of the most important tools you can have in the quest for your own inner freedom, although there are others, such as keeping healthy boundaries and choosing happiness.

But what is a frequent reaction when we get hurt by another in a relationship? We resolve never to let that happen again. We resolve this perhaps with a stiff upper lip or with bottomless resentment welling up inside of us. Either way, what we are doing is looking at the other as the fount of our pain, rather than - as said above - looking at ourselves. And so when we find that next relationship, we keep a portion of ourselves in check. We ensure that we will never again allow ourselves to get hurt. What kind of a relationship do you think will ensue? Clearly it will *not* be a relationship that brings about joy and growth. Instead, it will stunt and blunt and eventually - although not in the ways you are attempting to protect yourself from - you and your partner will both be hurt.

Comfort Zones

Who doesn't know someone who seems to be afraid of showing their emotions; who may be very caring and giving on other levels, but who just can't manage any real "feeling" words and actions?

Frequently these are men and women who may hide behind the cover of continual work commitments, who have a multitude of friends (often of their own gender) with whom they insist on spending a great deal of time, or who simply always maintain a veneer of reserve, even with their closest and dearest.

So you can never really get close to them. They simply don't let you. And it's almost impossible to have a conversation of any emotional depth; it may feel like struggling to grasp a slippery, wet fish if you try talking about emotions with them.

If you are feeling a vaguely uncomfortable twisting in your solar plexus, or a prickly tremor of warmth running through your chest and heart region, or your face heating ever so slightly as you read this, or when another person - especially someone close to you - attempts to have a conversation about emotions with you, most especially about *your* emotions, then you might recognize yourself as one of those individuals who remain in the emotional comfort zone.

The drawing below depicts the idea of the stagnation and lack of growth inherent to the comfort zone beautifully. *

Any comfort zone exists *in order to maintain the status quo.* That is, you keep it up so that different areas of your life remain under control, that nothing changes, and that you feel secure. As you leave your emotional comfort zone, you begin to feel twinges of fear because you are entering unknown territory where you run risks, most particularly of becoming vulnerable, of needing, and ultimately, of getting hurt.

What is actually happening is that by braving out into the uncharted wilds, by feeling the trepidation and fear, *you are granted an invaluable opportunity to discover new facets of yourself, to enrich yourself, and to stretch and grow beyond your present limits.* Thus did Columbus discover the New World, so did man step on the moon, and so can you begin to express emotionally.

Not risking stepping outside the comfort zone in matters of the heart; always taking the safe road, looking for paths you are familiar with all spell the death of emotional growth and innovation. They also signify an unwillingness or fear of looking inward, because to do so is automatically a step outside of the boundaries of the comfort zone. Where, but in the confines of the not-yet-explored self, will we find such riches? Jung wrote: *There is no coming to consciousness without pain* and Joseph Campbell was to echo that later with these words: *The cave you fear to enter holds the treasure you seek.*

Pulling Up the Drawbridge: There's No Way to Cross the Moat

When our comfort zone is narrow, and when we decide not to expand it, in particular when someone who has entered our life has scratched at the outer edges of that zone, making us feel the familiar fear (which we may explain to ourselves as *someone wanting to take over our life*), we may pull up the drawbridge, making it impossible to cross the moat in order to get close to us. Pulling up the drawbridge, or *closing our heart*, means that once again we have closed ourselves off. This applies not only to others, or perhaps one specific other, but also to ourselves. As long as we fear emotional involvement (and write it off as something else), and as long as we refuse to allow ourselves to get emotionally involved, we will not easily connect to our inner self. The moat without a drawbridge serves not only to keep others out, but also ourselves.

It's not difficult to understand the origin of this problem. Another matter is solving it. As small children we give our hearts easily and willingly. Generally our parents are the first people we give our heart to, or to whomever it is that spends most of their time taking care of us. But it is in the confines of this early relationship that we can find the seed of the adult relationship problem.

Am I saying it is the fault of our parents? Not necessarily. It might simply be the mistaken perception of the child that believes subconsciously and subliminally that love is painful. And even if it were the fault of our parents, we would then need to examine (with compassion) how they themselves grew up, and what happened to *their* hearts at that early stage of *their* lives at the hands of their own parents, and so forth.

In *Rewiring the Soul* I briefly described early childhood attachment theory espoused by developmental psychologists John Bowlby and Mary Ainsworth. It basically states that depending on the degree of safety and security a child feels due to its relationship with its primary caretaker in the early years of life (and this of course depends largely on the self-awareness that same caretaker has, the sense of inner security that caretaker has, and the relationship that caretaker has with his or her *own* emotions), there will be a greater or lesser degree of comfort in close relationships in later life. Much has been written about this, and recently clinical psychologist David Wallin has written a marvelous book for clinicians called *Attachment in Psychotherapy* in which he suggests methods and techniques for other therapists to use in their work with those clients who come with relationship difficulties primarily based on those early years. A brief section from *Rewiring the Soul* about attachment theory follows:

The relationship with our primary caregiver in childhood, that is, the main person or persons who are in charge of taking care of us, is largely responsible for how our attachment bonds are formed. By means of an experiment in which children are brought to an office or lab – a place that the children have not been before, and then briefly separated from their parents, developmental psychologists have concluded that there are four main types of attachment that impact our psycho-emotional health, our adult relationships, the manner in which we love, or do not love ourselves, and of course, our concept of ourselves. These are:

Secure Attachment

These children explore happily while the parent is still in the room, they get upset when he leaves and are comforted when he returns. They also know they can count on the parent for comfort when they are upset because of the way the parent normally responds to the child. If a stranger comforts them while they are upset, they respond well, but clearly prefer the parent. This parent responds well and lovingly to the child at all times.

Avoidant Attachment

These children explore, but not in connection with the parent. When the parent leaves, they are not upset, nor are they happy when the parent returns and if the parent picks them up they turn away, and show little reaction. If a stranger tries to connect with them they react in a similar – avoidant - fashion. The kind of parent these children have does not react in loving and helpful ways to the distressed child, and further, has shown the child that he prefers the child not to cry and furthermore, that independence from – and not need for - the parent is a desirable trait.

Ambivalent / Resistant Attachment

These children distrust strangers, become very upset when the parent leaves but cannot be consoled when the parent returns. There may be low maternal availability in the home or the parent may be inconsistent between appropriate and neglectful behavior. In other words, the child lacks consistent loving reactions from the parent and hence does not know what to expect, which in turn causes him to not know how to react.

Disorganized Attachment

These children have a lack of clear attachment type. When the parent returns to the room, the child may freeze or rock itself. The parent may be frightened or frightening, may be withdrawn, intrusive or abusive. Because the child feels both comforted and frightened by the parent, it becomes confused and disorganized in its attachment.

If the attachment bond we formed with our parents was not secure, there is a reasonably high chance that we experience some – or much - difficulty in loving the self. This will negatively impact our adult relationships as well, until we seek conscious awareness.

The less securely attached a child was in his early life, the more he will balk at close emotional ties, or the more he will be at great odds with those ties, even if he/she opens his heart to them. The work of the therapist is to find ways during sessions to offer a new road (in the safety of the therapist's office: that protected, sacred and holy place that Jung called the *temenos*) to that security that was missing in early life in the relationship with the primary caretaker. This of course implies that eventually the client will find that safety and security within, and once it is located there, it can no longer be threatened by emotions in the same way it is continually threatened as long as the client is seeking safety and security through the relationship with *another* as opposed to with the self.

Back to our moat. If we become aware of pulling up our drawbridge on more than one occasion; if we become aware of feelings of discomfort when we begin to get too emotionally close to someone, or they demand greater emotional closeness from us and we find such a request unreasonable, then the fact that we are becoming *aware* of this is telling us something about ourselves. I remember an instance of a female client who was in a relationship with a married man. He seemed to always hold her at arm's length, and her pain at this distance from him was always at the forefront of our sessions. Nevertheless, when he left her for another woman, although ironically, he continued to live with his wife, my client eventually found another man - who was *also* married. This clearly demonstrated our principle of insecure attachment leading to such *dis*-ease, or lack of *ease* in close relationships. She was far more comfortable with a man who was not truly available for her than she would have been with one who made emotional demands on her.

And so we return once more to our moat. We are uncomfortable around our emotions. We are uncomfortable around the emotions of others. We may find that the only time we find it easy to display emotions is when we watch a movie or see something sad on the news because in both instances the people involved (movie actors or hungry children in a sub-Saharan country) have no personal connection to us. Are you recognizing yourself?

Clearly this is a reality check. As you become aware of this difficulty with emotions in yourself (supposing it applies), are you willing to assume responsibility for doing something about it? Are you willing to recognize that precisely this difficulty is what can not only lead you to greater relationship heights, but can also lead you to greater inner well-being due to a heightened sense of inner safety and security - in your relationships and in your whole life?

Jumping Off the Precipice of Trust

Trust is an issue in the best of relationships. We must trust when we do not know what our partner is doing, we must trust when we do not know where and with whom our partner is. We must trust that our partner will not spill our deepest secrets to the world, and above all, we must trust that our partner will not deliberately harm us.

Quite another aspect of trust is the trust we have within ourselves in the knowledge that *no matter what happens*, we will be able to deal with it. In other words, we trust our innate ability to maintain our inner balance and a modicum of well-being despite outer events, *no matter what.*

But this latter kind of trust, of course, generally only comes after quite some acquaintance with pain, particularly the pain that arises in most relationships at some point or another. And that implies that in order to actually allow ourselves to enter those relationships that come *prior* to having achieved inner trust in our own ability to quickly find inner balance, we must somehow be able to trust the other. Because if we don't, we will either not enter new relationships, or only enter those that seem secure (we have the upper hand), or that offer another kind of compensation (such as a woman marrying a man, some generations ago - and perhaps even today - that will clearly provide for her financially, but may not be faithful, and whom she does not necessarily love). *Real* trust in an - as yet unknown or unproven partner - exposes us, may well make us vulnerable, and presents us with genuine emotional risk.

Another issue to contend with in the trust arena, is the fact that we may have been burnt once or twice, and have now decided (and you can read about this type of decision in hundreds and thousands of forums all over the world by disgruntled, hurt, deceived, disappointed, and abandoned lovers) that we will *never* again allow someone the possibility of hurting us that way. You know the all-too-familiar story.

But that is *precisely* the wrong way of going about this. Hardening the heart against vulnerability, trust and a new partner will either forever keep us from a truly emotionally satisfying (and growth-producing) spiritual partnership, or will throw us unwittingly back into precisely the same type of painful thing again, because we have not examined what happened, except under the out-of-focus microscope of blame.

Blame, as already addressed in this book does not allow us to grow. It keeps us forever anchored in a high-security prison with fortified walls of steel until we decide to look at matters differently. Whether we were badly treated by the partner that brought about the pain is not truly the important question. Much more important than that is whether we have decided to look at what it is in us that leads us into those relationships and then to take the decision - from a position of awareness - to tackle that part of ourselves in order to grow beyond that place in our lives so that we no longer need to face that issue in a subsequent relationship.

The 'thing' that lives in us that brings us into relationships that create pain in our lives, is not something we need to blame *ourselves* for either. None of this needs to be about blame at all. Not blame with regards to the partner, nor blame with regards to ourselves. It needs to be about growth and self-understanding. That can *only* happen if we chose to become aware.

Recognizing That Growth May Come About Though Vulnerability

We've already said much about vulnerability. Its most important element is the fear we may feel when we contemplate being vulnerable in a love relationship because that fear may ultimately wake us up to the recognition that precisely by walking towards the fear, we may overcome it.

> *What is needed, rather than running away or controlling or suppressing or any other resistance, is understanding fear; that means, watch it, learn about it, come directly into contact with it. We are to learn about fear, not how to escape from it.*
> Krishnamurti

By embracing it, it may become our friend. By courageously looking it in the face, it will help us grow and in the growth, it will help us connect to our own emotions that for so long we have held at arm's length, just as we have held those others who wish to be part of our emotional lives at arm's length.

Vulnerability and the fear that often accompanies it can become our friends as long as we are able to give the possibility that they may form part of the Ariadne's thread that can lead us out of the labyrinth a chance.

There are a number of typical scenarios in which people begin to experience the fear of becoming vulnerable (although it should be stated that at times these very same scenarios contain quite legitimate reasons for someone with a healthy connection to his or her own emotions to decide to cut off a burgeoning relationship):

Because I begin to feel too good when I'm with you - there's danger there

Teddy and Charlene started seeing each other and a few months later Teddy realized that Charlene possibly came closer to being his ideal woman than any he could remember. She was classy, elegant, intelligent, independent and sexy all in one package. She seemed to understand him very well, and he found himself more and more comfortable speaking to her about almost any subject at all. And she seemed to think the world of him. She was tender and loving and quite clearly found his company immensely enjoyable.

So what went wrong? Teddy found that the more he enjoyed being with her, the more he started feeling antsy. Something in his gut told him that danger lurked just around the corner. He knew the feeling from somewhere and he was not about to wait for disaster - emotional disaster with *his* emotions winding up in the wringer - to happen. And so he began seeing her less, avoiding her calls, and most of all, he began seeing someone else, because he knew from past experience that the new woman would take his mind off Charlene.

Clearly Teddy's early attachment process with his parents or one of his parents had been fraught with some kind of difficulties. Whatever Teddy had experienced in those initial years of life, it had caused him to regard emotional closeness as a warning sign for danger. And he acted upon it each time he felt it. The only times he actually allowed himself to enter into relationships was when he felt that he had the upper hand: financially, emotionally, intellectually or sexually, or a combination thereof. In other words, he allowed himself to enter committed relationship status, when he was *certain* that his partner would not abandon or otherwise hurt him, because of the partner's greater need of him than his need of her.

One final point: almost all of this took place subconsciously. It was only in therapy, when Teddy's relationship patterns were being analyzed, that he saw it. And it was only then that he had enough awareness to be able to make a conscious choice about the new direction in which he could tread.

Your desire to connect with me makes me feel suffocated

April and Matthew met shortly after his 29th birthday. Matthew was unlike most of the men April had met before because he seemed to be so very much in touch with his own emotions - perhaps a bit too much. However, at the beginning it was a pleasure to speak to someone who was so open in so many ways that involved himself, his emotional self and his inner self. He was so obviously willing to share those parts of himself, as opposed to tightly guarding himself against opening those doors.

At some point there came the time - and in hindsight April was able to pinpoint the moment precisely to the weekend they went away to celebrate her birthday - when he clearly wanted more from her on that emotional level, and began to openly ask her to share of herself in the same way he was doing. She parried and sparred as much as she could; protecting herself from these emotional demands, but Matthew became more and more insistent. As he did so, April began to feel he was suffocating her with those demands, and very shortly thereafter began to stop seeing him as much, stopped taking his calls, and one day simply told him that she had moved on.

And she felt so relieved when she did so, as though she had escaped from a spider web. But who was the fly and who was the spider? Once again, in the case of April we have someone who must have had early attachment issues with one or both of the parents. What those issues were is much less important than the fact that April needs to be able to begin to see in her relationship patterns (also see the chapter on patterns) that while she very much basks in the early glow of emotional sharing on the part of a new partner, she always balks once demands are made of her to reciprocate. And interestingly, she tends to do quite well with partners who live in another city, or even another country, or with partners who are married, although in those instances she will often refer to her regret that the relationship cannot prosper further due to geographical distances or prior martial commitments.

Your desire to connect with me makes me believe you want to control me: Version A

Spencer and Liz had met at a summer party in her brother's house. Spencer was ten years older than Liz and they soon started seeing each other several times a week. She was perhaps slightly more taken with him than he with her, but all in all they seemed to be very happy together. Since Spencer had a much larger home than Liz, when they spent weekends together, they would go there, and soon Liz began pointing out things that could be done to make the place more amenable, more efficient and above all, more feminine. Spencer began to feel the first twinges of discomfort.

Although Liz worked in a high-profile real estate agency and was considered very successful, in particular given her age, she tended to be less deeply involved in her work than Spencer, who was an investment banker. And so it happened that Liz began calling Spencer more and more often on the days they did not see each other. She simply wanted to connect, say hello, and perhaps mention whatever she had been doing that day, and in all fairness, did not in fact call more often than once a day, but Spencer began to feel that she was checking up on him. It came to a point that he asked her to stop calling him so frequently because combined with the changes she kept suggesting for his home and then the calls, he felt she was trying to control him. She retreated slightly wounded, at his clear rejection of her greater attempts at intimacy, and he began to feel guilty. That made him feel even more controlled, and so he began to back off, and finally told her he wanted to cool it.

The relationship was over. Spencer's early home life had included not only a very domineering mother, but also a mother who was not the best at making him feel loved and secure. For him Liz's behavior - while he did not necessarily recognize that parts of it reminded him of his mother - took him to an emotional danger zone and so he fled. Without awareness, and the *desire* to grow, this will never change.

Your desire to connect with me makes me believe you want to control me: Version B

In this case it's not only your desire to connect with me, but the fact that you seem to be leaving your life aside in order to spend time *only* with me.

Julia and Antonio met when they were already in their 40's. Both had been in several unsuccessful long-term relationships although Antonio bemoaned the fact that he simply couldn't understand why, because he had always given his all to his partners. When they met, both had been alone for several years. Julia was a professional body builder who took her work very seriously and Antonio was a journalist for a local paper who had begun working out at the gym where Julia trained. Julia was often out of town and when they met, Antonio had been working on a major national story and therefore was only in town on weekends for the first few months of their relationship. However, when he finished the story and returned home full-time, Julia began to realize that he no longer showed any real interest in his friends nor in any other activities she had believed he participated in, and only wanted to spend time with her.

At the beginning, no doubt a part of her was flattered, but she soon realized that more than being a delight, his need for her presence was becoming a burden that made her feel guilty, angry, suffocated and pushed all at the same time. The more he insisted on spending greater chunks of time with her, or on traveling with her when she had weekend shows to attend, the more she pushed him away.

His reaction was to become very sad and depressed, and he would often ask her what was wrong, because all he wanted was to be able to love her. Eventually, of course, this sent her over the edge and she ended the relationship.

It may be very easy for you to objectively recognize the dysfunctionality of Antonio's reaction in this relationship, but if you had a bird's-eye view of Julia's past relationships, you would see that Antonio's desperate and unhealthy need for Julia closely mirrored the behavior of her other partners. So the question becomes: why did she attract that kind of partner into her life? Or: why was *she* attracted to that kind of partner? Did she never see the early clues to what was going on? Was she totally blind to it? And if so, why?

One possible answer is simple: if we look at partnerships through the spiritual window, as situations in our lives that have the potential to help us grow, then obviously we must have as partners *precisely* those people who will most bring up our own issues *through their individual issues.*

Julia initially believed Antonio was an emotionally independent man, who spent much of his time away due to the article he was working on in the early months of their relationship. She did not notice - in those early days - that he rang a bit too often because in those days she enjoyed the attention because he was far away and could not make demands on her. She also did not notice that when he spoke to her on the phone, he would often mention friends and activities, but when he was actually home, he never spent time with any of those friends, nor participated in any of those activities. She simply wrote it down to a desire to be with her, bearing in mind they had little time, as she also trained many hours every day. And so, the part of her that actually feared emotional closeness and the vulnerability that accompanies it, was not alert to any of the needier characteristics of Antonio until he returned home for good. She ended the relationship, feeling he wanted to control her, feeling manipulated, and feeling totally justified in leaving him. And Antonio, of course, believed that once again, he had given his all to someone who simply could not appreciate the extent of his love. Both these individuals need to come to awareness about themselves if they ever wish to participate in a truly fulfilling and growth-oriented spiritual partnership.

My body is giving me a bad feeling

Perhaps it is just my body that is telling me something and none of the above described patterns have even entered my mind - but what my body tells me makes me feel very uncomfortable around you indeed. It is so very important to begin to become aware of these messages and to pay attention to them.

Some examples of the language our bodies speak when this kind of bad feeling arises are:

- a twisting in the gut
- acid in the gut
- palpitations
- a tremor
- a shift to shallow breathing
- halitosis (bad breath)
- increased perspiration even though there has not been an increase in temperature
- body odor even though you are wearing deodorant
- a lump in your throat
- a need to continually clear your throat, etc.

(Please note that these symptoms may also appear for totally different reasons, i.e., they are not restricted to relationships that make you fear being vulnerable or uncomfortable. They may also occur in relationships where you are overly *needy* in which case these physical reactions may be felt based on the resentment you feel because of the mere "crumbs" you are thrown by your partner, which furthermore causes you to despise yourself.)

And because I feel this way around you, the physical discomfort eventually becomes strong enough for me to end the relationship, although I may never have understood that this discomfort rests on something about you making me fear being emotionally vulnerable or makes me despise myself for my acquiescence in the face of your rejecting behavior because I have never closely examined myself. What could have served as a tool for growth was discarded - as it must be, if awareness has not come to form part of our daily practice.

It should be pointed out that in all of these examples, the scorned partner may *also* have issues of his own, based on the premise that if he were attracted to these particular people who have fears of vulnerability, he himself has issues that tie in closely with that. In other words, by not having his emotional demands fulfilled, he also may come to a recognition about something in himself that will permit him to grow, if he so decides.

It also needs to be reiterated that most of this is not conscious - on *either* side. The person who has neediness issues tends to only see that they give it all and in exchange receive mere crumbs. And of course, the person who has vulnerability issues *recognizes* a feeling; an uncomfortable, or perhaps even scary feeling that has *nothing* to do with the adult, and everything to do with the child that this adult once was. In the recognition of the feeling, which tends to be subliminal, the adult only knows that there is something about the partner that is suddenly no longer good because of that feeling. If the feeling begins to arise more and more frequently, he decides it is the partner's fault, and therefore he needs to move on *in order to get rid of that feeling*, never realizing that the feeling arises from his own connections to difficult emotional attachments from his earliest childhood and that the occurrence and repetition of those body-rooted feelings is the beginning of the possibility to resolve them once and for all.

*I am unable to credit the image on page 94 as it has been found on countless web pages with no reliable original source.

Chapter 6

Having the 'Talk' (Even If Your Partner Isn't Reading This Book)

Please note that I have decided to use the slightly more awkward 'he/she' and 'him/her' throughout this entire chapter, because I feel that if I refrain from that for greater ease in reading (and socially acceptable norms in regular syntax), due to the potentially contentious nature of this chapter, it might appear that blame is mainly being placed on the masculine components of our society and relationships, and that, of course, is far from the truth.

Having a talk with your partner where you spell out what you believe might bring success to the difficulties you two have been experiencing when you communicate, is one of the most proactive and immediate things you can do for your relationship. If your partner then recognizes the opportunity and agrees to participate in the venture, you will both find yourselves on the road with much potential for a new kind of partnership. (And if your partner does not yet wish to participate, you can begin this process on your own and perhaps by observing your strides forward, he/she will change his/her mind).

In order to ensure that the 'talk' you will have with your partner is as productive and successful as possible, it would be a good idea to read this chapter several times, not because I don't believe you're intelligent enough to understand it in its entirety the first time, but because you simply aren't going to remember everything after one reading (and remember that in some ways this is akin to learning an entirely new language), and it will depend to a large degree on your *knowing your material* prior to beginning the talk, whether or not it will have a positive outcome. You don't want to be saying in the middle of it if your partner asks a question: *oh, I don't remember, let me go and check the book.*

And of course it's not a question of you saying everything the way I suggest here at all, but that you have the general idea firmly planted in your head. If I may use a simplistic analogy, you know exactly what a kitchen requires to be minimally functional. Hence, if you had to explain such a room to someone from another planet, you would have no difficulty in doing so, even if they had never heard of a stove, a refrigerator, or a sink. It was Einstein who said: *If you can't explain it simply, you don't understand it well enough.* And if you want to bring about change in your relationship by getting your partner on board for at least some of the ideas in this book, you will need to know what you are talking about in easily understandable terms. (Should your partner be willing to read the book him or herself, then everything may be a lot easier.)

Being Conscious

In Chapter 4 we already addressed the topic of being conscious. It is also the main underlying theme of *Rewiring the Soul*. Therefore I will be brief, but I need to reiterate just a few points.

The *talk* that the title of this chapter refers to is essential to coming to some kind of evolution in your possibly and probably still not very evolved relationships, otherwise you would likely not be reading this book (I refer to relationships in the plural, because although I will be referring to your 'partner', this entire process can evidently also be applied to *any* fractious relationship in your life at all: your children, your parents, a friend, etc.) But to have the talk (which will be thoroughly described in the next section of this chapter), at least one of the two partners of a relationship needs to have taken some steps towards becoming conscious.

A part of you is probably already well along that road of consciousness, simply because you have made it this far in this book. If not, you would have given up, or thrown it away, or otherwise convinced yourself that this subject matter - and what it demands of you - is just not right for you. (And that, by the way, is also OK. We each have our own time and our own way. All roads eventually do lead to Rome.) Here is what is minimally necessary:

- An inner agreement with the idea that *you* are responsible for your own happiness and inner well-being.
- An inner agreement that along with that responsibility comes a need to continually be alert so that you *remain conscious*, otherwise, you will not be *able* to take said responsibility for your own happiness and well-being.
- An understanding and agreement that this need to be continually alert must be *nurtured* by some kind of practice, whether that is meditation or mindfulness or anything else that works for you. At this point you may merely be putting up post-it's on your bathroom mirror, computer monitor and fridge reminding you to be aware and awake, but whichever part of the voyage into the self you are on, you will have come to this understanding that it needs to be nurtured. Just as a plant does not flourish without good soil, water and sunlight, so also your awareness and state of being conscious will not flourish without some kind of reminding, nurturing and practice.
- Furthermore, an understanding of the basic premise of this book (not original to this writer) that relationships serve the greater purpose of allowing us to grow, precisely due to the miscommunication, stress, suffering and pain they bring into our lives. Understanding this greater purpose means that you are capable of viewing relationships as spiritual partnerships, as opposed to blithely assuming your relationships exist to make you happy.
- This leads you to the concept that accusations and blame and all the other negative reactivity we tend to have in our relationships will - ideally - no longer form part of your life,

or at least, that you are in the process of making this a firm goal and consciously attempting to put it into daily practice.

- In order for this negative reactivity - within which you have probably lived most of your life - to start changing into evolution-oriented growth and therefore non-reactivity, you will not only need to change your own behavior, but you will at least need to attempt to share all your insights with your partner and let him/her know how things will now - potentially - be different on *your* side. And how he/she might - should there be willingness and openness to this whole subject - also participate. Hence the 'talk'.

What is the Talk?

For some people this talk is perhaps the first time they have truly communicated. Real communication also takes place when we discuss the mortgage, the kids' education, work, needed repairs on the family car, who takes out the garbage, shall we bring your mother to live with us, and the next vacation, but that kind of communication about events and things is a different kind of communication than the one where both partners discuss emotions, vulnerabilities, fear and so on, that all emanate from their innermost selves.

So let's assume you, the reader, are the one who is preparing to have this talk. And let's assume that your partner has not read the book, nor, perhaps, is your partner a person who is really *into this kind of thing*. Because if he/she were, you would probably already have discussed the book with him/her, long before coming to this section on the talk.

So imagining that you may have to start from zero, I would suggest you first think of a type of situation or situations in which your partner typically accuses *you* of something or blames you for something (and jot these sample situations down on a piece of paper, as you will need them when the time comes to prepare for the actual talk). Here are some examples from other couples that may serve as a reminder about your own:

- you never take out the garbage

- you never want to watch what I like on TV
- you get so jealous over nothing
- you're always trying to tell me what to do
- you never listen
- you always contradict me in front of the kids
- you always shout at me
- you never hug me
- you always put me down in front of our friends
- you always tell me how useless I am

Armed with a list of the above nature - obviously whatever applies in your particular case, which may look very different from the samples in this list - you first need to realize that if you want to get your partner on *your* side of this talk, where you will be talking about a number of things your partner has possibly never discussed, let alone *thought* about, you will need to disarm him/her by talking about what *you* have been doing wrong in *his/her* eyes, or put another way, the kinds of situations between the two of you where *you* have been *reactive* instead of evolution and growth-oriented in the past. In other words, you will be pointing a finger at yourself and *not* at your partner in the course of your explanations in the talk.

This is very important. Even if, in your mind, it is generally your partner who does the 'bad' stuff, the inconsiderate stuff, the attacking, the shouting, the denigrating, the blaming, or giving you the silent treatment or - even when something is truly wrong - blithely telling you: *no, nothing's wrong. Why would you think something is wrong?* - you still have to start your talk by pointing the finger at yourself. Otherwise, your partner is going to take this as simply another attempt on your part to show him/her how wrong he/she is, the way you always do, and so will then stop listening to you, will stop hearing the *true intention* of your talk and will have made up his/her mind long before you get anywhere in the talk, that you are just out to make him/her feel bad. And by the way, choose things to point the finger at yourself where you are, in fact, in some part of yourself, in agreement with your partner about your behavior, i.e., it's really not necessary to resort to shouting or name-calling, or it really would be nice to learn how to be a bit more spontaneous in the hug department. If you choose things your partner accuses you of that you totally disagree with (i.e., *you always disagree with me in front of the children*, but in fact, it only happened that one time, two years ago at Christmas and you immediately realized it was wrong to do so, and never did it again, but it keeps getting thrown in your face, then don't use that particular situation. *That* would be a bad example to choose), you would not be able to offer your partner new ways of reacting in future, simply because you wouldn't be in agreement with potentially being in the wrong.

The next thing to do with regards to the list of things that *you* do (according to your partner), is to offer the new way you will wish to tackle them from now on. Prepare yourself to give very specific examples of your prior reactive behavior and your new growth-oriented behavior that you will strive for. (You will find numerous sample situations in Chapter 7.) Remember: no one is expecting you to be perfect, simply to try your best, to remember, and above all, to not lose yourself in the world of reactive thought where you are no longer conscious. So, if you flip back to page 110 to re-read the section about being conscious, you will need to become very serious about nurturing your practice of remaining conscious. If you don't, it simply will not work. You have to keep a handle on yourself. Remain aware.

Another thing about this talk is that it is a good idea to go into it well-prepared. You might take some notes before you sit down to have it, you might jot down a few bullet points on a scrap of paper, because what you don't want to do is get lost in the forest and no longer see the trees because of something your partner might say or object to in the middle of the talk. You need to stay on track. You need to know *what* you want to say and basically *how* to say it and how to reach your goal of spelling it all out. The *what* comes in the next section. The *how* will depend on you and the manner in which you and your partner typically speak to each other. In other words, this is not about me putting words into your mouth, but about presenting you with concepts and ideas, so that you may then put together the words to suit your particular situation.

One point that has arisen frequently when I recommend having this talk is that some people fear it. They worry about what the partner will think or say. They worry the partner will put them down for even wanting to talk about things in this way. They also worry it may simply cause another fight. Precisely because of this last worry is why I suggest that you focus the talk on *your* negative reactions about some things in the past, things your partner has complained about, or brought to your attention, so that your partner doesn't feel you are using the talk as an excuse to once again bring blame and fault to his/her door.

Nevertheless, it *is* true that the talk sometimes causes problems. This is something you will have to inwardly prepare yourself for. Think of some possible negative reactions that could arise, despite your best intentions, and in that case, either think of ways of smoothing them over, given what you know of your partner's character, or at the very least, be determined that *nothing* will make you break into reactivity, where you simply find yourself accusing or blaming or shouting. Keep an index card in front of you at all times where you can see it with words of the following nature printed on it: "Remember to stay aware and remember to CHOOSE not to react badly." If necessary, leave the room, but *only* after first saying something along the lines of *I need to cool off, so I'm going to take the dog for a walk (or water the garden, or check my email), and I'll be back in a while so we can continue talking about this.* You will have to be the one to take the reins of the situation that is threatening to come unraveled into your own hands and calm things down - not only in the room between the two of you, but more importantly, inside yourself. If this should indeed come to pass, use the moment as an opportunity to hone and exercise those new skills you are beginning to practice.

Another thing that may happen is that you prepare yourself for this talk in the way described, and that you then start procrastinating. Not necessarily because you are lazy or because you typically procrastinate, but because the thought of having the talk causes a slight twisting or uncomfortable feeling inside of you. Remember: whenever you do something that takes you out of your comfort zone, away from the status quo, you feel a certain amount of fear or stress because you are stepping into unknown territory. But without such stepping out, or crossing thresholds, the Gutenberg press would not have been invented (*nobody* wants to read books - people don't even *know* how to read), the New World that Columbus discovered would not have been found (at least not in 1492: *are you crazy? The world is flat!*), Neil Armstrong would not have stood on the moon in 1969 saying: *That's one small step for man and one giant step for mankind* (how ridiculous, *of course* it's not possible to fly to the moon), the internet would not have been invented (whatever for? People will never be able to have computers in their homes!) and so on. So, remember: crossing thresholds, even if it gets you ridiculed, or even if it is scary, often leads to great things!

Goals of the Talk

Here are some of the things you will be looking to achieve with this talk; some of the goals you will need to set in your head prior to having it, as well as understanding that achieving some or all of these goals will mean that things will have a very realistic chance for change in your relationship:

- Inform your partner about the main ideas of this book regarding *another way* of living your relationship; a way that would mean that you would communicate better and argue a whole lot less. It would improve the level of love and affection between the two of you, and it would ultimately mean that much greater harmony would exist between you.
- While it would be magnificent if you could inform your partner about the spiritual nature of relationships as detailed in this book, it may be too early for that. You must be the judge of that, because it is much more important to get your partner on board with regards to how you two could proceed differently, more proactively, and less reactively, than to get your partner on board with regards to this being a spiritual issue. That can come later.
- Inform your partner about your desire to improve your relationship, but that even though you are very aware of the fact that you are at least as responsible as he/she is for the problems you are experiencing as partners, you will need his/her support in order to make things better.
- Repeat to your partner that you are well aware that in order to have reached the point of difficulty you two are having

(whatever point that may be), *it takes two*; i.e., you hold yourself just as accountable as you hold him/her.

- Be able to inform your partner of your *own* intentions with respect to how you (ideally) would like to behave from now on when issues between the two of you arise, and be able to give specific examples of this. (See the next chapter for more detailed information and ideas about this).
- Be able to inform your partner of how he/she might be able to react / behave in future when those same issues arise.
- Inform your partner of some built-in safety measures - for both your sakes - that could be implemented *by either of you*, should the need arise (see below).

Some Guidelines for the Actual Talk

Decide to have the talk at a time when all is well between the two of you, with no specific issues marring your relationship on that particular day. Choose a time when your children (if you have any still living with you) are asleep or at school, preferably even deciding to hold the talk at a public place, a restaurant, or a café, so that both of you have strong reasons to remain calm and serene, no matter what happens.

Try to have the basic content of the talk completed in a maximum of 10 - 15 minutes. This is not so much about *convincing* your partner, as about *informing him/her* of your plans. Greater details can be discussed over time, as issues arise, as you manage to actually show your partner your new behavior - or not - because you need to understand that you *will* forget to implement the new behavior sometimes in the heat of the moment, particularly due to lack of practice. No one expects you to have this down to polished perfection - it will be a learning curve in awareness and accepting self-responsibility for both of you. Above all, you don't want to overwhelm him/her with a great deal of highly detailed information on that first talk about it all.

Start by mentioning that you have often wished that some of the problems the two of you are having could be eliminated by the wave of a magic wand.

Ask your partner to hear you out, indicate that the whole thing won't take very long, and then, if he/she has questions, promise to tackle them at the end.

Now tell your partner that you have been reading a book; (a book that you perhaps know that he/she may or may not 'like' in its entirety, but you need not say this at this point in time), that contains some positive ideas about how relationships can be improved.

Point out that the main reason both of you tend to have communication difficulties when issues arise, is because one or both of you:

- loses it
- starts shouting
- starts insulting or belittling
- refuses to listen to the other
- keeps interrupting the other
- walks out
- resorts to manipulation
- pulls out the silent treatment

And quickly follow up with the fact that it might not be extremely hard at all to change that, if *both* of you were willing to stick to some guidelines (try not to use the word 'rules' because that word - for some people - smacks of domination and control).

Mention that to a large degree this is learning how to make different choices than the ones *both* of you have been making up to now. If both of you can choose to stand back from your anger at the moment you feel it erupting or flaring, if both of you can choose to *intend* to do this *prior* to getting into difficult situations, then when the issues arise, or the buttons get pushed, at least a part of your brain will already have had some inner dialogue about this. Making new choices is most definitely not going to happen immediately just because you both agree it would be better to do so, because old habits truly do die hard, but having the intention to do so, and then consciously paying attention to what is going on *inside of you* (and your partner inside of him/her), will go a long way towards making this possible.

Should your partner interrupt with questions or objections, gently ask whether it would be acceptable to park those questions and/or objections to one side in order to keep on track with what you need to say, and then address all of the rest later. Make a point of specifically asking if that is ok. Try not to be impatient or annoyed. You want him/her on your side in this talk. You want him/her to see how hard you are trying to improve this relationship so that he/she will perhaps also have the same desire.

Now comes the part where you mention some of the typical situations where *you* tend to behave in ways your partner has mentioned that could be improved. Here's where you go back up to the 'What Is the Talk' section of this chapter, and choose several (two to three is probably enough) pertinent examples from the ones you jotted down earlier.

Point out the type of situation, point out *your* typical reaction and behavior, and point out how you intend to react differently now.

However, even though you are using a couple of examples where you point the finger at yourself - for reasons discussed earlier in this chapter - it is nevertheless important that you let your partner know that this is not about *you*. It's about *both* of you, and *both* will have to implement changes if this is going to work.

In this next part of the talk, you will need to point out the fact that without *awareness* it will not be possible to achieve success. Tell your partner that the reason *you* (yes, *you*, I am again asking you to point the finger at yourself) have reacted poorly in the past, is because you have fallen into blind reactivity. Your buttons get pushed, and you react the way you have always reacted in the past. But with awareness, by remaining conscious of yourself, this will change. Not all at once, but in time. Right now you will not want to overwhelm your partner with a lot of - potentially - new words like mindfulness, neural pathways, and so on. All you really need to do is to get the idea of *being conscious* out there, and you might add the bit about having post-it's up on your bathroom mirror, computer monitor and fridge in order to remind yourself to remain aware.

Explain that just like changing *any* habit, this will take time, and at the beginning might seem as though no progress is being made. Mention that when you go to the gym to build biceps and triceps, even though you work out several times a week, no visible muscle growth appears. But after a little while, you do notice strength, firmness and then definition. It's exactly the same thing with this.

Mention that at the beginning there are four ways this can play out each time something sets one or both of you off:

- *neither* of you remembers to be aware
- *you* remember to be aware
- *your partner* remembers to be aware
- *both* of you remember to be aware

Say that being aware means that *there is a gap between the button getting pushed and the reaction*. In that gap - and in part due to an inner dialogue you should both start having - lies the existence of the possibility to make a conscious choice. And in this case the choice would be to react in a way that is *not* the way you habitually react in these situations. You would consciously choose to react in a healthier way: healthy for you, for your partner, and hence for the partnership.

Also explain that while you might remain conscious enough to *want* to make a different - or better - choice, it is possible that one or both of you is still far too angry about whatever it is that is going on, to be able to actually do that (make the better choice). *However*, you just might be able to hold on to yourself long enough to decide that at the very least you will not argue or shout or blame or belittle, but that you will ask for a time-out.

So now is also the time to talk about the safety measure I'm calling a 'time-out'. It simply means that whichever one of you *catches* him or herself first, assuming you are not yet in a place where you can move beyond this 'time-out' phase and literally have a new reaction, now says to the other something along the lines of: *I'm so very angry right now, but I don't want to go back to where I normally go because of how we then almost always escalate. However, I need some time away from you, so I'm going to go for a walk, or go up to the bedroom, or go for a drive,* or whatever seems appropriate. Add, to this, that you would, however, like to resume the conversation about the 'problem' a little later, when you have calmed down. And then go.

In the talk, as you are explaining the above point, you need to ask your partner if he/she understands the difference between 'walking out' on an argument, or refusing to address something, and this very different "time-out" phase. His/her understanding of and agreement with this is crucial, because otherwise by asking for a time-out in a heated moment, things might simply escalate. But by having had this talk, at the very least, your partner will know what is going on, and with which intention it is happening.

Another very important point in the talk is to mention the need for signs of some kind. Let's say you were to agree upon a sign such as the one the tennis referee uses in a match - also 'time-out', where the palm of one hand is placed on the up-spread fingers of the other hand. Or the sign could be something like both palms facing, hands held high, so that the other partner actually sees it. Because the need for this arises when *one* of the two has remained aware, and the other has *not*. So what happens is that the one who remains aware (and it might *not* be you), makes the agreed-upon sign *in order to make the other partner aware of the fact that things are escalating and that in fact, what had been agreed upon in this talk, is to try not to allow that to happen.*

This means that again, your partner *must* agree (as you also must and you should say so very clearly) to at least abide by the intention of this part of the talk, i.e., to *not hold against you* that you might be the one to do this (to make the signal) and especially, must agree that when the sign is made (if it were made by *you*), to not get even angrier. It might happen that in such an instance, the partner who is reminded about the escalation of emotions by the partner who has remained aware decides to take a time-out to cool off; i.e., go for a walk, etc.

You will also need to explain that this new way of reacting signifies that both of you will find new ways of saying things to each other. Imagine an argument starting. Buttons are pushed and tempers flare. But *one* of you remembers to be aware. That one might now say something like: *this is where we normally lose it. And right now I'm as angry (bitter, frustrated, sad, etc.) as I always am when we get here. But I really want to start talking in a new way with you, so even though I don't exactly know how we are going to solve this issue, at the very least I'm not going to make it worse by yelling* (or insulting or crying, or whatever you habitually do) *at you.*

I'm choosing to try to work it out differently. How do you feel about it? Now you see that this kind of talking brings the two of you to a different place. It's not yet a place where anything is solved, but it's a better place than the one where you normally get stuck and where things tend to quickly unravel. And now perhaps, the other partner will say something that further helps to de-escalate the situation which simultaneously allows the two of you to cautiously look at the situation with new eyes, and with greater willingness to resolve and greater readiness to see the other's point of view, and most particularly, a greater desire to find harmony *together*.

Remember:

- Always try to find a place of inner balance.
- When you behave better than usual, point it out to your partner, not only that you reacted in a better than usual way, but discuss how you would have normally done it, and that this time you tried to do it this *new* way. Make sure your partner understands that this isn't about you praising yourself, but about you using the situation as a learning experience for *both* of you.
- Praise your partner if the new way is chosen by him/her, especially when *you* forgot even if you have to bite your tongue. This is, after all, what you want. Your hard work is paying off!
- Your partner needs to agree to do all of this, or at least that he/she will try, and that he/she has basically understood and internalized what's going on.
- Even though this sounds like an awful lot of work and continual analyzing of everything, it's only like that at the beginning. You are building muscles for a new kind of relationship life - a spiritual partnership - and the day will come when all of this comes automatically.

Chapter 7

It Takes Practice!

In order to learn how to react in new and more evolved, growth-oriented, or spiritual ways when issues arise in your relationships you may benefit by hearing about some examples of how others have dealt with their problems. While your own situation won't be exactly the same, by studying how these couples have figured out how to re-engineer their reactions with regards to their particular problems, you may gain some insight into your own.

Remember that the fundamental points of the more evolved, growth-oriented, or spiritual ways of reacting in partnership are these:

- Remaining aware.
- Taking responsibility for your own reactions.
- Remembering to always seek inner balance *before* having any kind of outer reaction.
- Taking responsibility for your own inner well-being and happiness.
- Remembering to always love yourself (because a loving self will not wish to have reactions that make it feel terrible).

- Acknowledging that you always have a choice.
- Acknowledging that when your partner pushes your buttons there is at least a chance that the main reason your buttons are getting pushed, and that you are on the verge of having an emotional reaction of some kind, is because something about what is happening touches on an issue of your own.

When you or your partner *do* remember to be aware, and *do* remember to react in a new way, after you have both talked about whatever the issue was, or perhaps the next day, it would be a good idea if you each congratulated each other on a job well done. Understand that this changing of a life-long habit is not so terribly hard, but it is *only* possible if you make a firm practice of the intention to be aware and then do all the rest. *None* of it is possible without that. And so of course you both deserve praise along the way for the times you actually manage to do it.

And let me reiterate that you would do well to remember another thing, especially if you are beginning to think that your life is going to become one analyzing session of each other's reactions after another. *It will not!* This will only need to happen at the beginning. Much will become quite obvious after a while and will no longer require anything other than intention and attention although you may still find that it is interesting to discuss what just happened.

So now let's have a look at some possible situations that can arise between partners (of any gender):

Jealousy

Melanie and Bob went to a party together. Melanie flirted outrageously - or at least that is how it appeared to Bob. He kept watching her out of the corner of his eye and she was continually chatting with the host's younger brother who looked like he'd walked in from a Calvin Klein men's commercial. Bob felt heat in his face, he also felt a stabbing in his heart, and he didn't know if he was going to shout at Melanie when they went home or if he was going to give her the silent treatment. But Bob was the one who had read this book. And Bob was the one who had held the 'talk' with Melanie. Bob managed to regain a certain amount of awareness before actually getting into the car on the way home, so he decided to talk about it with Melanie in a different way than he might have in the past. He first asked her to hear him out without interrupting because he was going to try to put some of the elements of the new way of reacting into place, but that he was finding it very hard. Then he told her that he was very upset due to what he had observed at the party. He felt that Melanie had let him down and made him look foolish in front of the other guests by spending so much time with Tom's younger brother. He asked her why she had felt it necessary to do that, and furthermore, why she had laughed so much while she was doing it. Was Tom's younger brother *that* funny?

As he spoke, it was clear that Melanie understood that Bob was trying hard not to react the way he usually did, because she kept taking his hand and stroking it. When he finished, she said that she understood why he had thought she was flirting with Tom's brother, but as it turned out, he had been telling her about how he had proposed to his fiancée, who had not come with him this evening, because she was out of town on business. Apparently everything had gone wrong when he proposed and in the end it had just become a huge joke, although his fiancée had said yes to the proposal.

After Melanie finished telling all of this to Bob, she stared at him, and asked him if he realized that normally he would have shouted at her for doing something he *assumed* she had done, without waiting to find out what had really happened, and in return for being shouted at, Melanie would have given *him* the silent treatment, or, if he had chosen the silent route himself, she might have wound up apologizing for something she hadn't done just to get him to stop the silent treatment and talk to her again.

It's important to also examine what might have happened if Bob had simply gone into reactive mode in the car, and Melanie had been the one to remember to be aware. If this would then jog him into awareness, then things would also be ok, but if he would refuse to go down that road, perhaps because in the anger or pain of the moment he was unwilling to go there, then it is still very important the Melanie does not lose her own cool, but that she recognizes that this particular situation will need to be re-addressed at a later time, perhaps the next day. At that point it is possible that Bob might be willing to discuss matters more calmly.

Blaming

A dripping faucet didn't let Kathy sleep all night - again. Christopher had promised to fix it long ago. Promises keep getting made, Kathy keeps believing them, but eventually she starts out most days by blaming Christopher for one thing or another that is somehow connected, although mainly in her mind with a broken promise. Christopher feels Kathy only focuses on what is wrong and never on what is right, and so constant low-grade bickering arises between the two of them which leads to a general state of discontent on both sides. Both sides feel aggrieved, unjustly maligned (Kathy, because she feels she has a right to blame - after all, promises have been broken; and Christopher, because Kathy never seems to appreciate any of his good points, she only sees what is wrong), and so everyday life has spiraled down into something rather miserable between the two of them.

On this particular morning, Kathy wakes up with a headache from having slept badly due to having been kept awake once again by the dripping bathroom faucet. And so, as she comes downstairs, she sees Christopher drinking coffee and reading the newspaper, and she immediately lashes out at him, asking why he hasn't opened the curtains. As she pours herself a cup of coffee, irritated that he had not left it on the hot plate meaning it is now lukewarm, she opens the refrigerator only to find there is no milk. Christopher was to have bought some the evening before on his way home, but he forgot and used up the last of the milk for his own coffee.

And so Kathy loses it, and starts shouting at the top of her voice, one accusation after another, blaming, blaming, blaming. Christopher - to whom Kathy had given the 'talk' several days ago, makes the agreed-upon signal that means he has remembered about the talk, i.e., he has remained aware enough to do so, instead of going into his reactivity which is generally to hunch his shoulders and weather it out, in the best of cases, and in the worst, he would simply walk out of the house without saying a word, not letting

Kathy know where he was, sometimes for more than a day, which tended to terrify her, and it was his way of calming the situation down.

Now, however, he reminds her of the talk, quickly adding that he believes she is right. Mollified, Kathy does not get upset by being reminded that she forgot to be aware, and that she had fallen into reactivity. Now Christopher confesses that he hates having broken promises to Kathy as much as she hates him breaking them. He hates the consequence: Kathy's rage. He says he knows he has never taken responsibility for those parts of himself, and that while he does not know whether he will soon have a perfect record, he vows that he will now take it much more seriously than he has in the past.

But if Christopher had not remained aware enough to remind Kathy about the talk, and about what they had agreed to do, or if Kathy had not been willing to take a step forward into awareness when Christopher reminded her, then both would have likely fallen back into reactivity. Nevertheless, hopefully one of them would remember (that neither had remembered at the moment of the argument) perhaps later that day or the next one. Once that happens, *it is very important that the partner that remembers this, take the initiative to have a conversation about what happened.* If this is not done, you're not getting any practice at all. You should discuss what happened, if perhaps there was a moment when either of the two could have popped back into awareness, and even if not, to at least look at it dispassionately now, in the aftermath, with the hope that the next time, at least one of the two remains aware. And reiterate then and there, that whoever remains aware, when that one reminds the other, that then the other will accept this reminder and not use it to fuel his or her anger even more.

Belittling

Jacqueline, a literary agent, and Brandon, a professor of economics, had guests over for dinner. She commented that she had read an article concerning the global financial crisis and mentioned that Greece appeared to be nearing the verge of stepping out of the Euro Zone. Brandon started feeling embarrassed because their guests were much more sophisticated politically than Jacqueline, and he felt she might say something that would make her look silly, and so he interrupted, making a light comment about experts on modern fiction not necessarily being experts on world politics and finances, and turned to the guest at his right - a journalist specialized in investment banking - and asked him what he thought of the situation. Jacqueline let it pass, although she was seething, simply because she did not want to cause a scene in front of their guests - something which she knew Brandon was counting on - and so waited until they were all out of the house.

As she turned on him, eyes glaring, ready to let him have it, because he made a frequent habit of this in front of certain people, she could see that Brandon had a strange look on his face. He grabbed her hands. He said he was sorry. He said - it had been Brandon who had read this book and had suggested they begin to try to live their relationship differently, and it had been Jacqueline who had been very skeptical about it because of how set he was in his ways, according to her - that he had *just* at that very moment remembered everything they had discussed while they were having the talk. He told her he had forgotten. He said he knew that if she had done something like that to him in front of guests, he might have wanted to pour a glass of wine over her head.

Listening to him say these things, made Jacqueline soften and smile. But she said that it was one thing to be able to remember after the facts, and another to keep on belittling her in public. Brandon agreed. He also said he would practice becoming more aware - taking this whole effort more seriously.

Is this couple out of the woods just because of a small moment like this? Of course not. However, because of this brief interaction where Jacqueline has had a glimpse of a man who was sincere in his recognition of his part in the problem, and invested in making it change, she will most likely also begin to look at whatever she does that bothers Brandon, but more importantly, they are now both invested in beginning to communicate in a new way, of which they have just had the barest glimpse.

Shouting

As Susan is tidying the kitchen after dinner she asks George to take out the garbage. They had long ago agreed that this was one of his chores. The next minute George starts shouting at Susan and tells her that she *always* has to say something just before he is on the verge of doing it. She will never trust him, he says angrily, to do it on his own without her interference. Rage makes George's face very red as he continues. Susan's immediate reaction is to shout right back saying that last night and the night before that, as well as many, many other nights, *she* was the one to have to take out the garbage, simply because George never respects his part of the deal. But she manages to catch herself. She is, in fact, extremely angry, because she feels he is being so unfair. However, due to her desire to respect the guidelines of the talk they recently had, after both having read this book, she tells George that she needs to have some space, that she is going to go for a walk, and that she would like to talk about it all when she is more calm, maybe in a couple of hours. George looks surprised, he had clearly forgotten about being aware, he seems to be relieved, and nods his agreement.

Later that evening George pours both of them a glass of wine and they decide to sit out on the terrace in order to talk about their barely-avoided fight. George begins by apologizing for shouting, but more than that, expresses regret that he forgot about being aware and having a choice about his reaction. He also states that he is very relieved that Susan remembered to be aware and that therefore they have managed to avoid the fight. He tells Susan he does not believe they have yet solved anything to do with what started the potential fight, but that he is very pleased that they are talking about it in this new way.

Susan seems gratified and agrees. She tells George that she appreciates that he did not get even angrier than he already was when she told him she had to go for a walk to cool off.

But now they have to discuss the real problem. The garbage. Or, better said, the points they had agreed on when they decided that each of them had certain chores concerning the upkeep of the house. Since both work, there is limited time to do this. Perhaps they need to work out a different list of tasks, or a different schedule.

But they will also need to discuss some peripheral matters: George is perhaps very sensitive to Susan's implied criticism and Susan is perhaps overly quick to jump the gun when she believes George has not performed one of his agreed-upon tasks in a timely fashion. Perhaps George needs to take on greater responsibility for his part of the agreement and Susan may need to be more circumspect in the way she addresses what she may consider to be tardiness in the tasks. Perhaps they need to agree that as long as the task is completed on that day, but not necessarily right after dinner, that it is acceptable to both.

Whatever the case, what becomes clear by examining the problem in this light, is that it is a question of talking about it calmly, and then *both* parties assuming responsibility for whatever aspect of it that they have agreed to. This responsibility, taken on by *each*, is crucial to the success of this new way of reacting. Even if a couple manages to get to the stage where they are capable of speaking calmly about issues that might have caused explosions previously, if one of the two neglects his or her own responsibility in then fulfilling whatever has been agreed upon, things will unravel again very quickly because such neglect of the individual responsibility then appears not only as disloyalty to the partner and to the agreement, but also - and this is perhaps much worse - as a direct challenge to the agreement and to the potential for harmony in the relationship.

Controlling

James knows that he is more than just a bit of a control freak. He likes things to be just so. When he goes on vacation with Natasha, he makes certain that all plans are 100% pre-selected, pre-booked and totally confirmed. But life happens. Suddenly something slips out of his control and a plane departs so far off schedule that they miss their connecting flight and have to find an airport hotel (which they may *not* be reimbursed for), and that makes him feel terribly out of control. He become anxious, stressed, and his immediate reaction is to make those who are closest to him tremble with his outraged frustration.

Natasha is used to it, she has learned to stay out of his way when he gets like that, but at times she simply hates that he seems to have no control over his emotions. On those occasions she goes silent, and if he asks her what is wrong, she says that nothing is wrong, but clearly something is. She may take several days to stop being like that. Evidently this mars that special time spent together, but obviously - at least at first glance - James plays a large role in this as well.

They have just started a long awaited vacation to the Seychelles. James has spent an inordinate amount of time preparing for the trip, and everything is organized with fine-tuned detail and precision. They miss their connecting flight in New York City due to poor weather in Cincinnati, their city of origin. The next flight they can be booked into leaves nearly 24 hours later, it is winter in New York, they have practically no cold weather clothes with them, and to compound the frustration, their luggage is lost. James begins a tirade with the airline counter agent, and when he returns to Natasha to tell her the negative outcome, in a rage, he remains aware enough to notice that she is shutting down as she occasionally does when he behaves like that. Somehow he manages to change his reaction immediately *because he was aware.*

She was the one who had read the book and told him about the talk, and although he did not delve into it, he liked the idea of using difficult moments in the relationship to grow, so although they had not in fact, had any practice, he remembered it, and began by apologizing. He told Natasha he was very sorry for taking his stress out on her, and that he was willing to do whatever it took to make sure that she did not withdraw from him the way she sometimes would.

That led to a surprisingly insightful comment by Natasha about herself. She told James that she believed she would sometimes withdraw because she felt that his behavior was so outrageous and unacceptable, but because she did not have the courage to say so, fearing he would get even more enraged (not at her, but at the whole stressful situation), that she would shut off and in the process shut him out. In a way, she felt, it was perhaps a bit of passive aggression but mainly a lack of guts. This, of course, is a case of unhealthy boundaries on Natasha's part, and of trespassing boundaries unashamedly on the part of James. They did not necessarily know enough about the intricacies of psychology to call it that just at that moment of time sitting in JFK airport, but they both felt enormous relief suffuse them simply because of this brief conversation that came about thanks to a moment of awareness that was willingly taken advantage of.

An aside must be made here. At the moment of awareness that James experienced in the midst of his outraged frustration at the airline, the weather and the baggage handlers, he had a choice to make. The choice was to remain aware and to address Natasha in this new way. *But he could have chosen to react the old way, or continue reacting the old way, despite his momentary awareness.* And in fact, this does often happen at the beginning when people are trying to react in the new way, but something about the old way of reacting is stronger. Part of it is habit, but another way of explaining it is by referring to it - in Eckhart Tolle's words - as the pain body, or in Chris Griscom's words, the emotional body.

What follows is a brief reproduction of what I wrote about it in *Rewiring the Soul:*

Here is how Chris Griscom wrote about the phenomenon in the eighties (in *Ecstasy is a New Frequency*):

"The seat of the emotional body is the solar plexus chakra, which is in the area of the stomach. Our emotions are registered by the solar plexus ganglia, which trigger the sympathetic nervous system of fight or flight. This alters the blood chemistry in the brain, and the vagus nerve activates physiological responses which actually carry with them an electrical jolt. Everyone recognizes that jolt from experiences where they were taken by surprise – the massive surge of fear and anger which brings us instantly to attention. The jolt spreads itself out in widening arcs which characterize disillusion, shame, and anxiety. *The emotional body becomes addicted to these jolts. It begins to seek people and situations which will re-echo the original charge, even though we become desensitized or unaware of it on a conscious level."* (italics mine)

And this is Eckhart Tolle's take on it well over a decade later (in *The Power of Now*):

"As long as you are unable to access the power of the Now, *every emotional pain that you experience leaves behind a residue of pain that lives on in you.* It merges with the pain from the past, which was already there, and becomes lodged in your mind and body. This, of course, includes the pain you suffered as a child, caused by the unconsciousness of the world into which you were born."

"This accumulated pain is a negative energy field that occupies your body and mind. If you look on it as an invisible entity in its own right, you are getting quite close to the truth. It's the emotional pain-body. It has two modes of being: dormant and active. A pain-body may be dormant 90 percent of the time; in a deeply unhappy person, though, it may be active up to 100 percent of the time. Some people live almost entirely through their pain-body, while others may experience it only in certain situations, such as intimate relationships, or situations linked with past loss or abandonment, physical or emotional hurt, and so on. *Anything can trigger it, particularly if it resonates with a pain pattern from your past.* When it is ready to awaken from its dormant stage, even a thought or an innocent remark made by someone close to you can activate it." (italics mine)

And there is something else about it, something perhaps even more powerful. The pain body or the emotional body is seductive in its pull on you. It is addictive. You *want* to go there. You want to *stay* there. By going there, you somehow feel right, despite the pain, somehow vindicated, despite not being able to change that painful past you are reliving, and by staying there you are able to see over and over again, in your mind's eye, in your heart, and in your tears, exactly what happened, how it happened, and how, because of how it happened, *you are right in reliving it.* In other words, you tell yourself that *you have a right to* your anger or your pain. Something happened or was done to you that justifies that you continue to feel this way. *If you did not feel this way, it would almost be as though you were telling the world (or yourself) that whatever it was that happened, was not so bad. Feeling the pain, wallowing in it, over and over again, gives meaning to the event. And the event must be meaningful, because it was so painful.* I imagine that you can see how this is, in some fashion, a catch-22.

Now let's return to the moment of awareness that is or is not chosen. If it is not chosen, and if James had gone back to the old reactivity, generally we could say that the emotional or pain body has stepped in and taken over because it still has an incredibly strong hold on the person. A part of James might wish to react in the new way, but another part clings to the old one for all the reasons indicated in the above section: familiarity, wallowing, justification, etc. *So there has to be a conscious battle* to win this thing. And the conscious battle takes place in the person's mind, with some self-reflection and inner dialogue. *Do I want to win this or not?* And it may take several tries. It is not necessarily going to come as easily as described here in the example with Natasha and James. But one thing is certain: it *can* be done.

Manipulating

Ginny has plans to go out for dinner with her girl friends. In fact, this is something she and Blake had agreed upon some time ago: they would each have a night out on their own every couple of weeks (or even more often). She would go out with her girl friends, and he would see his football and poker buddies. It would not be the *same* night, because one of them has to be at home with the kids. The problem is that it's actually Ginny who hankers after this bit of fresh air and freedom more than Blake, and so when the night arrives, all manner of things happen. Blake often sighs and comments: *I really don't understand what you find so great about having dinner out with your friends* and then turns around and sighing once again, says: *I guess I was raised to believe that your family is enough for you.* Now Ginny feels guilty.

Then he says: *but don't worry, I'll get the kids their dinner and then I'll work on the awnings for the garden terrace because we didn't get around to it last weekend, but I don't mind doing it on my own, and it will keep my head focused.*

Now Ginny feels even more guilty. And slightly angry. More than angry, she feels resentful that because Blake doesn't care about spending some time away from her, he always makes her feel guilty when *she* wants to do it. So she does it less and less, but feels more and more resentful. Often on the day after her outings, she and Blake fight about nonsense but in her heart she knows it is related to the fact that she went out, that he felt abandoned and unloved and that she feels resentful.

So on this occasion she goes out and decides - consciously - to have a good time and not feel resentful, but determines that on the following day she is going to have a talk with Blake about this. When they get up the next morning, things start off on the wrong foot (as they tend to do) and he criticizes the way she cooks breakfast for the children, and does so in front of them. She decides to grab the bull by the horns and asks Blake - who is a real estate broker - whether he has clients at lunch. When he says no, she suggests they meet for lunch at a place halfway between her own office and his. He looks surprised, then worried, but quickly agrees.

At the restaurant Ginny immediately gets to the point. She reminds Blake about having discussed the 'talk'. She says that when he gently complained the night before about her going out, he made her feel resentful. And then when he criticized her cooking in the morning, she wanted to hit him on the head with the frying pan! She suggests that since the nights out are such a bone of contention, they need to discuss the topic in new ways, figure out some kind of solution, because clearly neither is she going to want to stop having them, nor is he - unless they figure out how this can be changed - going to stop feeling neglected or abandoned on the evenings in question.

He offers that he feels she doesn't love him, when he sees how much she enjoys her nights out. He just believes that if she really loved him, she wouldn't need those nights out on her own. (For the skeptics among my readers, please believe me that there are plenty of people of both genders who feel the same way Blake does, and it often has little to do with demographics.) He adds that when he goes out he simply misses her and wishes he were back with her.

Ginny doesn't really know what to do with this, but asks Blake if she can be totally honest. On his nod, she says that when he talks like that - about thinking she doesn't love him just because she wants to see her friends, and about saying he just misses her when *he* goes out - that she feels suffocated. She adds that it seems as though he *needs* her too much.

You can see what is happening here. This couple is having a very different kind of conversation because one of them remembered to be conscious. They are thinking about their relationship, themselves, their reactions and the current issue of going out on their own every so often in very different ways than in the past. They will need to explore all the possible roads this new conversation has opened up for them carefully. They may want to get some relationship coaching or therapy. They may want to simply practice and practice and then practice some more being conscious and aware as much as possible every single day. But if they stay on this new level of thinking and reacting, they will have an excellent chance of beginning to see their *own* issues and perhaps beginning to deal with them, instead of blaming the other and feeling bad about something.

Neediness is involved here, which implies an important lack of healthy self-love that will need to be addressed, trust issues are involved, patience, recognition that relationships often benefit from some 'being apart' time, but perhaps it is also very important for both partners to recognize that while they may not always agree totally with the desires and wishes of the other, because they love each other, they can be capable of simply letting the other one do what they believe they need to do in order to be happy. This can be a delicate line, as it might sound as though I am proposing that partners step all over each other's boundaries, but I am not. This simply means that occasionally partners choose to disagree and yet support each other in the disagreement and obviously continue to love each other. This requires much aware emotional and psychological maturity that will pave the road towards spiritual partnership.

Criticizing

Mark is driving the car. Jennifer can't stop telling him what he's doing wrong. She insists he's not careful enough, he's too slow, he's too close to the other car, why doesn't he overtake the other car, he drives too close to the curb, he always goes through yellow lights, he doesn't come to a full stop at the stop sign, he grinds the gears, etc. It most certainly doesn't take anyone very long to understand why Mark is ready to let Jennifer have a piece of his mind. That would be his habitual reaction.

He glares at her angrily as they stop at a red light and opens his mouth, but Jennifer interrupts. She tells him she forgot to remember to be aware. She wasn't thinking about their talk. She had decided earlier to not have a go at him again like that, but in the moment had simply gone into automatic pilot and had started criticizing the way she always did. The light turned green as she put her hand on his knee and said that nothing had really changed in the way she thought about his driving, but what was beginning to change was her recognition that it was totally horrendous of her to behave that way with him.

Mark couldn't believe his ears. He said he appreciated what she had just said but that he was very, very angry about all her criticism and that he did not think that he was capable of talking about any of it at that moment, because what he really wanted to do was to throw her out of the car. But he appreciated her intention. Could they simply not talk until they got to where he was dropping her off and then perhaps have a conversation about it that evening at home?

Jennifer was amenable to the suggestion although she really would have liked to talk right then and there, especially because she was so proud of herself for having remembered to be aware.

Again, in this example, by mere virtue of the fact that Jennifer was able to stop the ball rolling on in the direction it always rolls, means that this couple will also be able to discuss the matter in a new way. How they reach a solution is not so much the point of this particular example, as the fact that by consciously stopping a blind reaction, communication on another level can begin. This is worth gold.

However, if you think that when they *do* talk about it that evening, they will just get embroiled in an argument as they generally do, you *might* be right. But they have a real chance of not going there. He might start by telling her just how humiliated he feels every time she criticizes his driving. She might answer by saying that she simply had no idea that it affected him that way; that she merely thought she was pointing out a potential danger. Nevertheless, she might add, that now that she sees his point of view, she wants to deeply apologize (sometimes the best way of beginning one of these talks is by apologizing; sometimes a good way is by explaining how such-and-such, when it happens, makes you feel) for having created such terrible feelings in him.

That might lead to a talk about boundaries - Mark might say that angry though he would get about her words, he was never able to tell her that it was not acceptable. Or he might tell her that she made him feel like a little boy the way his mother did when she would criticize the way he did his homework, or whatever comes up because these kinds of conversations tend to take a couple into territory they have more often than not never previously explored. Therefore such conversations can be of great help in their understanding of each other. And of themselves. And so it allows them to grow. They grow as a couple and as individuals. And that is a wonderful beginning of a new kind of relationship - a spiritual partnership.

Needing to Be Right

Cheryl tends to go to bed a bit earlier than Jonathan. He lets out the dog for a late-night constitutional in the garden and then, on coming back into the house, slams the door - and this almost *always* happens. This results in Cheryl - who is a light sleeper - waking up and then she has a very hard time falling back asleep. She mentions it - once again - the next morning. Jonathan insists that it did not happen. He adamantly says that she is simply wrong. They bicker. It goes back and forth, but Jonathan's insistence on being right does not change, and Cheryl knows that she was awakened by the slamming of the door. Her immediate reaction is to begin yelling because she is *so* frustrated. This happens over and over.

So on this particular morning when Cheryl comes downstairs, feeling wan and tired, and Jonathan is clearly cheerful and at the top of his game, she slumps into a chair without even getting her coffee. Jonathan, on the verge of touching her hand, asks her what is wrong, with a concerned look on his face, but backs away as she screams at him, asking what does he mean *what is wrong*, if he already knows that once again she hasn't slept and now is going to have an awful day thanks to his *usual* lack of consideration. As he stares at her and her anger, her motors are only getting started, and she takes a deep breath to continue, but suddenly deflates.

She asks him if he remembers the book they were reading together and the talk they had and that they wanted to start behaving differently. She says that she believes it will be very hard for her to stick to that agreement if she doesn't even see that he is making an effort. He starts to interrupt her in order to insist on his innocence with regards to slamming the door, but changes his mind and decides not to go there. Instead, he makes a suggestion. He admits that it might be true that he simply slams the door and is not aware of it because in his family everybody always made so much noise. He said that it could also be that because her sleep is light, that she wakes up from any ambient noise and then thinks the door was slammed. He suggests they get a new door that can't slam. He admits that this isn't actually solving the manner in which they react to each other, but for the time being it would allow her to sleep, or at least, if she still doesn't sleep, she would know she had not been woken up by the door slamming.

At this point in the conversation Cheryl seems to have perked up considerably *simply because for the first time in a long time* - at least with regards to this particular topic - *she feels she is being taken seriously.* That makes her feel better. And she says so. That makes him smile. She also says that the minute she feels she is being taken seriously, it's no longer so much about whether she is right and he is wrong, as about being able to discuss the matter in an acceptable way that will lead to change. Now the atmosphere between the two of them has changed energetically. This is good. And this is a good beginning for changing other reactions in other situations. They might decide to talk a bit about taking on responsibility for whatever each agrees to - he, perhaps agrees to take greater care with noise at night on a very conscious basis, and she, perhaps, agrees to be less belligerent, or to support him in his attempt to become more considerate in this regard by praising him when things go well and by being more patient when they don't. However they decide to deal with this particular point, they have realized communication is essential, but also as he learns to be more considerate and she less belligerent, they are actually working on their own issues and consciously growing towards a new kind of partnership.

Lying

Louis is very busy professionally and has numerous reasons for going out to dinner with business clients. However, Gloria knows he has an issue with alcohol (or marijuana), and when Louis wakes up the day after one of those business dinners, Gloria can tell that too much was consumed. When she asks about it, she is told that very little was consumed, and that she is being overly suspicious. But Gloria recognizes the tell-tale signs and thus knows she is being lied to.

And so she loses it. She loses her temper, her patience, and we might say, at least momentarily, she loses herself because of how she speaks to him as if he were a piece of poisonous waste that she has had the misfortune to step on. His shoulders hunch, he looks more and more chagrined, but keeps trying to convince her that he did not do what she is suggesting.

And then *he* remembers the talk. Worried that she will get even more upset, he nevertheless makes the agreed-upon time-out sign. He points out that she had promised that if he were the one to remind her to come back to awareness, she would not take it out on him. She stops mid-track, a furious look on her face, until she finally backs off, figuratively speaking, and sits down. But then she tells him that she sees no point in doing this if he is going to continue insisting on lying about the prior evening.

Now he sits down as well. He looks at the table. Then he looks at her. He says that she is always so perfect, she never gives in to temptations, she seems to have no problem in keeping herself on track, and he feels useless beside her. So he drinks (or whatever his substance is). It makes him feel better about himself. And yes, it's true, it happened again last night. And he *was* lying when he said it did not happen.

Now a look of utter amazement comes over Gloria's face. I just can't believe you're admitting it - just like that, she says. What's different is that you remembered to be aware even though I didn't and so you thought about what you were doing by lying. So now I have to tell you something too, she tells him, because I've been lying too. Maybe not by denying something that actually happened, but by pretending that I always have everything in the palm of my hand, and that I'm so organized and things just work for me. They don't. I mean, I get really stressed about everything and at the office I'm always yelling at the staff, and I'd actually like to get a prescription for a tranquilizer, but then I think about you and what you do with alcohol and how I'm always accusing you, and I don't want to be like you that you depend on alcohol to relax you and make you feel better, so then I pull back from getting the prescription, but then I get really resentful that you *get* to drink, but I don't get to take a pill.

Louis is so amazed and surprised at what he just heard that he has a reaction he would never have expected. He bursts out laughing. And so does Gloria. OK, they haven't solved anything yet, but again, as in so many of these examples, they've communicated and they've looked at themselves instead of pointing the finger outwards. And that is a big step in the right direction.

Sex

It was great when you first met. Now your partner seems to have gone cold on you. The truth of the matter is that your advances are greeted with anything but enthusiasm. You not only feel rejected, you feel small. You feel as though something has been stolen from you. The topic of sex becomes not only volatile, but downright explosive. You accuse your partner of being cold and your partner accuses you of being a sex addict. It always ends badly, and since it generally starts at night, it often means you don't sleep well, and so the next morning you feel awful when you get up to face your day. Because your immediate reaction is accusatory when your partner rejects you, or lets you know that your advances are not welcome, you know that it is precisely at that point in the interaction between the two of you that you will need to change something. (Much more about this subject in Chapter 8.)

Actually ... We Don't Fight ... But We Don't Have Sex Either

There are couples who essentially get along and live companionably side-by-side, but sex has also declined for them. Their process requires a search for greater connection by deliberately seeking new modes of communication that involve their inner selves to a greater degree than has happened to this point. They need to re-kindle the *interest* in each other (or perhaps, truly *awaken* it for the first time) and could begin by making weekly dates to see each other with no one else - and no television -

present (if money is an issue, it can simply be a walk in the park), where both firmly commit to beginning a practice of sharing topics of interest, ideas, feelings, thoughts and emotions that may have occurred over the past week. They need to *touch* each other on levels that they normally do not via these conversations. Genuine interest in what the other has to say needs to be present. A genuine desire to *share* also needs to be present. Initially nothing may appear to be changing, but with patience and perseverance it will. (For more about this topic, also see Chapter 9.)

****

There are many other potential areas of conflict that will need to be addressed in the new way the 'talk' proposes. Some of the most typical are:

- cheating
- harping on the past long after it's gone
- your (or your partner's) parents
- money
- kids

Many of these examples have several things in common:

- Poor boundaries on the part of one or both parties:
- Lack of awareness
- Lack of self-reflection
- Lack of self-responsibility
- Lack of self-love

In other words, what binds these examples together is precisely all that was discussed at the beginning of this chapter regarding the fundamental points of the more evolved, growth-minded or spiritual ways of reacting in a partnership.

Using these examples to motivate yourselves, being consistent and diligent in your practice of being aware and finding inner balance *before* you react, you *can* bring these changes about in yourself - and hopefully your partner will wish to be on board as well. Either way, you will have enriched your life immensely.

Chapter 8

How Does Sex Fit Into Spiritual Partnerships?

Let me say it in a nutshell: greater self-reflection coupled with greater awareness, coupled with greater connection between the partners in a relationship on the inner level such as this book is all about, are all hallmarks for a much deeper, richer and above all passionate sexual bond. Why? Because there is *connection* in a way that does not exist if we're mainly about what the two of us have as a couple - professionally, materially, socially, and even personally. There must be more if we wish to maintain great and vibrant sexual desire.

Passion - as most of us know - is not only brought about by beautiful bodies that bring chemistry to life. Nor is passion brought about only by love and need, although many believe that is how it should be and then find themselves astonished when that alone does not keep passion alive. Both men and women alike, although we're somewhat more used to seeing it on the part of women, often fall into the trap of seeking eternal youth in order to continue looking seductive, falsely believing that this will keep the passion in their relationship alive. Others believe that external trappings, such as designer clothing, shoes, handbags, jewellery, and even cars, are part of the mixture that will - if not guarantee - at least foment success in the passion department. And when it ultimately does not work the way they believe it should, they often seek more youth or greater external trappings, all in the hope that it will lead them to success.

Conversely, if we look at sexuality and the life of a couple's passion from the point of view of the love both partners feel for one another, we find that many couples believe that their love will sustain their passion over the course of their lives, *even when they have already been through one or more relationships where this did not happen*. They may tell themselves that it did not work because it was the wrong partner, or because their partner did not love them as much as they loved the partner, or because the partner was not - despite all appearances to the contrary at the beginning - as interested, in fact, in sex, as they themselves were. *So of course the sex had to die*. But this time it's different. There is something to be said about sexual energy and the fact that we fail to understand it at our peril.

How good is your sex life? How often do you have sex? Have you stopped having regular sex because you've been married 10 years and your partner is no longer particularly stimulating? Or have you stopped because he's in andropause or because she's in menopause and because you never were that crazy about it to begin with? Or maybe you stopped having it with your last partner, but then you found someone new where the passion came alive again and now the pattern is repeating, and it's stopped being exciting once more.

What does all this mean? And more importantly, what can you do about it?

The *energy* that is inherent in sex makes it a much more important aspect of our lives than mere pleasure, although pleasure is obviously a massively contributing part of it. Twenty-first century socialization is such that we are primed from early adolescence on to expect fireworks from sex. We believe sex will be one of the most vital and essential experiences of our life – *as indeed it can be*.

However, due in part to this socialization via mass media (movies, television commercials, and glossy magazine ads, to name only a few), we come to expect something of our sexual lives that simultaneously *increases* its importance on levels that are perhaps inappropriate, and *decreases* its importance in other, much more relevant areas. This ultimately creates a general population that is frequently dissatisfied with its sex life – but for all the wrong reasons, and without knowing what the solution could be.

What is sexual energy? Sexual energy is not only the passion that you feel (hopefully) as you engage in sex, but on other, much more transcendent levels, the doors that open energetically between you and your sexual partner during sex. This energetic exchange remains available for both individuals for a period of time after sex. Have you ever slept in the same bed as your partner and been drained the next day? Conversely, have you ever slept in the same bed as your partner and been refreshed the next day? If you are at all sensitive to the flow that can be established between two people after sex, you will have already connected the dots and realized that the way you feel the next morning does not *only* depend on expressed or unexpressed ardor, or the relative comfort of the mattress and the pillow, but much more importantly, on the energetic exchange between the two of you.

So how can this sexual energy be harnessed? If relationships are not transparent and if the partners have not learned to speak clearly, honestly, and openly with each other as discussed in this book, sex will almost always - ultimately - be negatively affected. If you do not speak about sex with your partner, you have little chance for the real energy inherent in it to come out. It may be wildly passionate for a time, but the energy you can access with it may not be available to you.

But pay close attention here: when it comes to the sexual aspect of a relationship, speaking about sex with your partner is not *only* what it is all about. You must also make the *conscious decision to want to grow together with your partner*. This mutual endeavor, via the connection you have (or are beginning to seek) through the relationship you share makes the difference between a relationship that may ultimately fail, or lose its fervor, and a relationship that not only has a chance at long-term survival, but also one that – because of the energetic connection inherent in sex – does not eventually flounder and die a slow death of sexual strangulation. The essence of conscious growth in a relationship depends on the couple's desire to grow together psychologically, emotionally, and spiritually. This implies, as so often reiterated in this book, conscious awareness of the self, conscious awareness of all one's feelings, thoughts, actions, and reactions as well as acceptance of the fact that each of us is responsible for all of these facets of ourselves. This conscious link between partners keeps sex alive in ways that go far beyond sex toys and fantasy games because it speaks to the *real – and eternal –* connection between the two individuals.

Let's go back to explore the concept of passion - that so frequently frustrates and eludes us - in order to better understand what it's really all about, how it works, and above all, how to sustain it over the life of a relationship.

Sex at the Beginning

Pure chemistry. Passion. Can't keep our hands off each of other. Heat emanates from one to the other, even across a crowded room. Others will sometimes comment that they feel totally excluded when the two who are in such a passionate, love- and lust-filled relationship are in close proximity. Many of us have been there. This is such an incredibly exciting, vibrant and fervent phase of a relationship. It may also border on obsession, need for possession, single-mindedness, where no one and nothing else comes into real focus. We may not feel a real need for eating and sleeping, almost as though passion were fueling us, giving us everything we need.

At this point, assuming it's more than a one-night stand and more than just an affair, it is invariably complex to ascertain where chemistry and lust end and exactly where, *if at all,* love begins. They are so profoundly intertwined and entangled that we may mistake one for the other, although this by no means signifies that real love doesn't exist. What is probably the case, however, is that we do mistake the connection that the chemistry gives us for another kind of connection that has *not yet been established* at all. And sometimes we mistake the chemistry for love.

Another element that comes into the equation is need. We believe we need the other because of how we are together sexually, and then we believe that this means that we love each other. While all of that may - on some level - be true, what is also true, or at the very least *probable*, is that again, we have *not yet even begun* to establish the kind of connection we will need to carry this relationship forward with success - most particularly and specifically in the arena of our sexuality. Am I stating that people don't give serious thought to their relationships and only commit to each other because sex is good? Of course not! But I am saying that passion and need are very powerful forces that can hold us in their sway, even if we are no longer teenagers, and that will color many of our decisions, despite giving those decisions a great deal of serious thought. We may try to protect ourselves with iron-clad pre-nups, specific clauses to financially protect the spouse who gives up a career to raise the kids, and so on, but none of this is the kind of serious thought this book is arguing in favor of. These are all *outer* circumstances and what the kind of partnership I'm proposing is all about, has to do with the *inner* circumstances of both partners.

Sex after the Beginning

The turning of the page into the next chapter of any relationship is as different as we are all different, and while it isn't invariable that the relationship has to end, because most of us know of couples who have been together for 40, 50 and even more years - and not necessarily in a bad way - what often does change markedly, despite continuing to include major elements of a loving relationship, is sex. It shifts, loses some of its erstwhile fire, gradually fizzles out, often requires something out of the ordinary to rev it up again, but even that doesn't always create the desired effect, and sometimes it fades into the woodwork, if not for both partners, then very often for one of them.

And while it is true that there are also couples who continue to have incredible sex - sometimes to such a degree that even if they divorce, they continue seeing each other for the sex *after* the divorce - what is frequently the case in such couples, if they open up to tell you what is in fact going on behind closed doors, is that while the sex is maintained, little else is. They have few subjects of real conversation, or few points of common interest, or they manage their relationship with a continual round of socializing or other kinds of incessant distractions that keep them from becoming too aware of the fact that the main pillar of their relationship is sex, but possibly little else. I can hear the comments coming in, saying: *well, having great sex is better than not having sex, I'd prefer not to have great conversations, but at least have good sex.*

When sex has begun to pall, people will typically tell each other some of the following, most of which are myths of some kind that get propagated by the media, our friends, and sometimes our friendly neighbourhood pastor or priest, the counselor we see, or other well-meaning people in our lives:

- sex never lasts
- if the relationship is good, you really love each other, despite only having sex once a month (some readers will protest and say it's actually only once every three or even six months or even less frequently)
- it's impossible for the kind of passion we had at the beginning to continue
- it means I'm no longer in love, because if I were, I would still desire my partner
- it means my partner no longer loves me, because if he/she did, he/she would continue to desire me

One of the greatest dangers of this chapter in our relationship life is the one-night stand, the fling, or the outright affair, each of which is, of course, a step along the relationship continuum in the direction of another individual with whom we can fall in love/lust instead of first looking at our current relationship.

When interest in sex has waned on the part of one or the other, the one who isn't getting any wants to know he/she is still attractive and desirable to others, and may be tempted to have a fling in order to prove *that*. And the one who no longer desires the partner may want to know that he/she can still feel that surge of passion, and may thus be tempted to have a fling in order to prove that. Sadly, *neither* 'proof' proves anything, other than the fact that you found another individual with whom you were able to have good sex. Period.

But it says very little about what is going on in your current relationship, and it certainly - at least most of the time - does *nothing* to resolve the problem facing you in your bedroom. It's a way out, especially if this is the first time you are confronted with this sexual enigma of waning desire, and furthermore, it gives you someone on whom to firmly place the blame - after all, if you are able to have great sex with someone else, it means there must be something wrong with your partner, right? Behaving and thinking like this is very human indeed, but it keeps you from looking at the real issue, which most often has little or nothing to do with passion and genitals and desire, and much more to do with a lack of real connection on another level that so many relationships simply don't achieve.

And let me re-emphasize - it's not a question of people lacking intelligence or willingness, but of not knowing. We are lulled into a kind of sleepy foolishness by society, mass media, marketers who want you to believe that you will be sexy if you wear this, look like that, drive this, drink that. We believe that our lives are to be lived on the outside and pay so very little attention, if any at all, to our inner life. I wrote extensively about this in *Rewiring the Soul* and only want to reiterate a point already made in an earlier chapter of this book: as long as we continue to live that way, focusing mainly on our outer lives, our relationships will tend to be destined to *be so very much less* than they could be, and that includes most particularly our sexual connection with our partner.

What would you do to have fabulous sex? Not this, you say? Not go inside? Not connect with the self in order to connect with *the self* of your partner? Not grow yourself in that inner direction? It doesn't mean not having your shiny toys, you know. You can still drive a fast car, have a well-paying job, go to 5-star restaurants or burger joints, fly commercial, take a cruise, fly on a privately leased jet, or watch an X-rated movie. You can still play poker, wear short skirts and six-inch heels, ski at a luxury resort, or watch chick flicks and action movies. *None* of those things in and of themselves are good or bad. What makes them one thing or another, is how much we need them, depend on them to feel good, crave them, feel we are better than others if we have or do them. But they are so very much *less* important than going inside and looking at the self in order to begin to truly connect to ourselves and our partner.

At this point in this particular chapter of the relationship where sex is often fading fast, the partners may also frequently start to play strange games. Most of these games involve emotional, sexual and even financial manipulation, because if indeed one of the partners wants more sex than the other, then he/she may believe that this (manipulation of some kind) is the way to get there. Some of these games have been described in Chapter 1 and you would benefit from having another look at them.

Another example of what may happen is portrayed in the following story which is, in fact, an amalgam of several stories. Philip and Liz had a mind-blowing passionate affair. After about six months they decided to move in together. Eventually they decided to get married. They were so much in love. It made sense to commit. But now, Liz, Philip's once passionate partner who desired him so much, doesn't want to make love anymore. She avoids him, she shuns him, and he becomes bewildered, self doubt arises in him, he feels hurt, unloved, and finally angry. So he leaves, or he threatens to leave, or he finds himself someone else who *does* find him desirable. Suddenly, magically, Liz wants him again. The passion is back. The old chemistry is flying once more. So then things settle down. Everyone is happy just like at the beginning. *But it happens again. Liz doesn't want to make love anymore.* What on earth is going on?

If you are a man, and you recognize bits of this story, when you were a child were you – in some fashion or another – abandoned by your parents (or by one of them)? Perhaps you were ill and had to spend a lengthy period of time in hospital. Perhaps your parents – and particularly your mother - were kind and caring, but you perceived that they simply did not love you enough for your needs. Perhaps you *yearned* deeply for a love that you were never given. Perhaps an event occurred while you were still a child, which caused you to feel rejected by your mother in a particularly important way.

If you are a woman, and you recognize bits of this story, when you were a child were you – in some fashion or another – abandoned by your father? Perhaps your parents – and particularly your father - were kind and caring, but you perceived that they simply did not love you enough for your needs. Perhaps your parents divorced and your father left and rarely saw you. Perhaps he was physically there, but emotionally absent. Perhaps he rejected you. Perhaps you felt he never gave you the approval you so avidly sought. Perhaps he (or another important male in the close family environment) abused you sexually, physically, psychologically, or emotionally.

Whatever the case, in the scenario both for boys and girls, the missing ingredient, or the essential point to realize, is that something has gone awry in the way the child views the love he or she receives from the parent. In other words, the child has not received – or perceived – a developmentally healthy *lesson* about love from the parent.

And what happens when you learn something incorrectly?

Think for a moment how you were taught how to hold a pencil when you were learning how to write. Most of us learned it properly. Some didn't and you can see it in the way they hold a pen, or in the way they scrunch their fingers together. How about when you learned how to slice or dice vegetables? Do you julienne? Or do you chop and cut a mess of unequal misshapen pieces? And what about how you learned how to use Excel or Word? Or sew? Or ride a bike? Or dance the tango?

So what happens when you learn something incorrectly? Don't many people continue to do whatever it is wrong again and again and again? Until something happens to make them want to change their method?

This is exactly what happens when a child learns dysfunctional lessons about how love works. The child continues to "do it" incorrectly. Why? Because he or she believes that that is the right way to have love.

So here you have a child who learned that love means getting hurt - whether the pain is in the heart or in the body is actually not so important. Pain of whatever kind hurts, and much of this kind of pain, however it originated, leaves noticeable psychological impressions and emotional trauma. But *before* the pain came, the child felt – even if only briefly – *real love.* The child experienced something that he or she believed to be the real thing. The love it felt for the parent was magnificent, the way love is meant to be, and the child reveled in it, the way most of us do when we feel we are truly loved and cherished. The child believed the parent reciprocated this love in the most wonderful and caring way. *The child felt safe. The child felt loved. The child felt secure.*

And then the blow fell.

Whether it came in the form of rejection or coldness or abuse or abandonment is not as important as the message the child gives itself in order to try to understand what happened. And although the content of this message may vary, with consequences of a varied nature, for the purposes of this chapter, the message the child gave itself was that *love is not safe. Love is dangerous. Watch it! When you feel truly safe and loved, something bad will happen.* And of course it's all subconscious.

Fast forward. The child is now a teen or an adult, embarking on a relationship, keenly interested in finding love, and frequently looking for it in the guise of sex. It is not unusual that this individual is – *or appears to be* - highly passionate. Sometimes this individual sees him or herself as more passionate than most other people. He or she may believe sometimes, somehow, that sex is love. And when this individual finds another person with whom the sexual flame ignites in the way of great passions, then typically, frequently, this person falls desperately, frantically, obsessively, fearfully, longingly in love.

All of the adjectives in the last sentence that describe the state of mind of our protagonist as he or she falls in love tend - in some unwavering fashion or another - to form part of the scenario which is now choreographed. A dance begins. The individual often shows him or herself as a highly passionate, highly sexual person. He/she shows boundless desire for the partner, particularly during the phase of the relationship where the partner is not yet quite committed. *None* of this happens deliberately, or in a calculating fashion. It is an unconscious pattern in which sexuality plays a leading role, but not a scheming mindset designed to *catch* an unwitting prey.

The less accessible the partner, the more highly the flames of passion will leap, and eventually in some cases, the couple commits to a life in common. They decide to live together, to get married, or even, in some instances, to commit by deciding to have a child or buy a home together.

So now our protagonist has achieved what appears to have been the goal: love, a committed relationship, a life together. Finally there is this long-desired state of love. Love is corresponded. A long awaited state of circumstances has arrived, and therefore now the two live happily ever after, right? Well, possibly yes, but not, perhaps, without first going through some tough trials that involve the most intimate aspect of the couple's bedroom - the sexual relationship.

Now a phase begins that is generally misunderstood by both partners. Neither can explain how this once passionate person quickly turns into someone who shuns the marital bed, making up the most ludicrous excuses to avoid sex, or, if sex continues to play a part in the relationship, the partner who is turning off, finds it more and more difficult to continue playing a role that is no longer tenable. In other words, the erstwhile passionate individual no longer wants sex. He or she may even find it disgusting, having a hard time keeping this fact from the bewildered partner, and frequently the turned off partner will do his or her utmost to make certain the partner does not know how much sex has become repulsive, because *love has not necessarily diminished,* and there is no wish to hurt the shunned partner further.

In the meantime of course, the confused partner suffers a gradually decreasing sense of self esteem, at least as far as his or her sexuality is concerned. He or she may believe that sexual desire and hence the frequency of sex has waned because he/she is less attractive, less desirable, or because the partner has found someone else. They may also believe that the partner has become frigid or impotent, indeed, the person who no longer wants sex may believe this also. Occasionally - as already stated - they may seek out a new sexual partner, just to convince themselves that they can still *function.* Many things are imagined, but the truth of the matter is rarely realized, *particularly not by the partner who has turned physically cold.* And the solution never lies in exchanging one partner for another, because invariably the pattern will repeat itself. Like most issues discussed in this book, this one must be resolved from within and not from without.

The truth of the matter – at least in some instances of the type of background described above – is the fact that the individual with the difficult childhood came to believe, back then, and on subconscious levels, that being safe in a loving situation is the threshold to some kind of pain - emotional pain, psychological pain, etc. When this person was a child, and when he or she felt safe and loved, something happened to cause this pain. The connection between feeling safe and loved on the one hand and pain or danger on the other hand, has been clearly established in the subconscious mind. So when this person finds him or herself in a safe loving situation, a type of inner panic button begins screeching a warning, albeit on subconscious levels, and something has to be done to upset the applecart and avert the danger.

This is the moment that some of the people in this situation turn "cold" on their partners and sex eventually goes down the tube. Almost as though by doing that, the connection between love and safety is successfully broken. They have been striving for just such a situation for so long, but nevertheless, they are sabotaging it in the most insidious way. Insidious not only for their partner, but also for themselves. And of course no one knows what on earth is going on. Typically the individual who no longer desires the other continues to love the other very much. At least for a while. He/she usually feels tremendously guilty about not desiring the partner. The other partner feels rejected, but the one who is off sex, in time may begin to believe that it's actually due to the fact that the partner truly no longer is desirable. Or that his/her personal hygiene is off, or that his/her love-making techniques are no longer interesting, none of which of course has any relation to the real reason. Ultimately neither partner is looking for the answers inside. Ultimately it is such a difficult situation that many couples just give up. The guilt and the inevitable hurt can grow to enormous proportions.

There are solutions. But I can't pretend they are easy. Or even that there are *always* solutions. The dynamics of this particular psycho-emotional dilemma, whose almost invisible tentacles delve deeply into an individual's sexuality, are difficult to disentangle. They require a great deal of awareness, not to mention patience and goodwill, not only on the part of the person who has gone cold, but also on the part of the partner. It would be a mistake not to recognize and understand that for some reason the rejected partner has also drawn this into his or her life, and so, on another level, this is a secondary dilemma that also needs to be faced, as already discussed at length in the chapter about relationship patterns. To be so rejected on this very intimate and visceral level of the marital bed, bears much examination, and at the very least, a strong sense of lacking self-love lies at the bottom of it (if we look at what 'issue' caused the rejected partner to be attracted to the other one), although other factors are most definitely also closely involved. Seeking the inner connection on a level of highly evolved awareness I discuss in so many parts of this book is - for the couple that finds itself in this admittedly thorny situation described - one of *the* most promising methods to resolve it.

If you are reading this and have recognized yourself or your partner, I urge you to seek help (therapy, counseling, or relationship coaching). Not because either of you is sick, but because this is a hard one to grapple with on your own. A very important element of the solution lies in removing pressure from finding the resolution as the solution is being sought. By that I mean that although the solution needs to be sought actively, it needs to be done in such a way that the partner who has gone cold *does not feel pressured to have sex for a time*. Another very important element is allowing love to live and flow in spite of the problem, in order that both partners realize that they are loved *despite* the problem. For some people, on the receiving end of the sexual coldness this may be impossible, and in that case, the relationship has probably come to an end. But for those who are capable of continuing to love, there is hope for the relationship, and *hope for the eventual resurgence of passion*. And finally, the most important element of the solution lies in psychological and emotional awareness on the part of both partners about the dynamics of what is occurring, and to recognize that love - especially when our early lessons about it have been dysfunctional - is both the cause of the problem and the solution to it.

****

When sex wanes or dies a slow death, clearly the problem is not always as dramatic as what I've illustrated here. Many couples remain together with little sexual satisfaction because they *do* continue to love each other and because they wish to maintain the family unit intact. Many such couples have passed through my office and there is a yearning, a lingering regret, about the fact that for them sex is no longer in the foreground, but they are not seeking new partners.

Precisely for that reason and to offer hope, this book is about some of the methods that can be used for the couple to find a passionate connection again by using the spiritual one. *Until we become conscious and begin to take responsibility for ourselves* we will continue to play out patterns in our relationship lives, and in those patterns elements of our sexuality are almost always included.

And part of that process of becoming aware and assuming self-responsibility concerns evolving the self by literally learning how to grow as this book describes through the issues that arise in our relationships and taking responsibility for the way we behave in those interactions with our partner. This offers the possibility of bringing us closer in unprecedented ways, and of reigniting our sexual passion. The new connections we make with ourselves and with each other bring this potential about. (More about connection in Chapter 9.)

Sex after the Talk

At the beginning, nothing much changes sexually. You're just barely starting to walk down this path that will change not only *each* of you, but will also change the relationship. The *main* difference at this point will be that you will both start to think about each other - and about yourselves - differently. You'll want to - if you remain aware and do this the way it's been outlined in this book - find growth instead of blame. You'll want to become more of what you are, understand yourself more, grow as an individual, love yourself more, and in the process you will begin to see your partner - who is hopefully doing a similar thing - very differently than the way you used to before. *This* - how you view yourselves and how you view each other; how you connect with yourself and how you connect with each other through this process of continually being aware with each other as you react to each other at all times - is what will change the relationship and eventually bring you both back to passion.

In this process of connecting with yourself and each other, many of the topics discussed in Chapter 3 begin to fall into place. One of the biggest is that we take on more and more responsibility for everything about ourselves, having realized that what occurs *outside* of ourselves should never have the power to wreak havoc in our *inner* world, if we have accepted responsibility for our inner well-being and balance at all times.

Sex at the Beginning of Connection

It may be tentative at first. You may both be somewhat suspicious of it. Or perhaps you find yourselves suspicious of the newly-found passion not lasting. You may be fearful, hesitant, timid, uncertain, surprised, gratified, hopeful, and elated, all in one fell swoop. It almost seems miraculous, perhaps even too good to be true.

Trust the process. Let it happen. Simply go about your days as you did during the earlier chapter of your relationship, right after you had the talk. Allow yourselves to grow as you continue to learn to react in awareness, as opposed to being blindly reactive, and in this growth, allow yourself to enjoy the wonder of the burgeoning inner connection with this human being who is - in some fashion - becoming a soul mate in ways you (and romantic novels or films) could never have imagined.

In this stage you will have setbacks. If you have been moving along well for some time in your new state of awareness as you react to each other, it is very possible that some old issues arise, or simply that new ones appear. Remember that as we climb a mountain, new boulders appear to block our path, new ravines emerge that need to be crossed or circumvented, and we may not find suitable shelter for the night, and yet we have to remain up there on the north face of that mountain, if we want to reach the summit. In our newly-emerging spiritual partnership it is the same. You can't expect things to always go smoothly, especially at this early stage. You have seen the greatness of connection, perhaps you have even glimpsed the divinity of yourself and that of your partner, and then, a few moments later, you find yourself mired in the muck out of which you thought you had ascended long ago.

Trust the process. Don't lose faith that what you are doing is the right thing. Talk it through. Perhaps you need to reiterate some of the points of the initial talk you had together. But know that you are growing, and if you *both* believe in what you are doing, this path will bring you back to passion.

Sex as You Are Growing

Now you know that passionate sex will be part of your expression of love for each other as long as you are together. You no longer entertain doubts about this. You know that your sexual expression does not depend on a youthful or fashionably dressed body, a specific way of moving or behaving, or on the newness and freshness of a relationship, but on the conscious love you have both grown into throughout the process of learning how to react to each other - and to yourselves - from a position of continual awareness.

Ironically, it is the *spiritual* aspect of your partnership that has rekindled the sexual aspect, fanning the flame of a passion that is immeasurably more than the one you knew before.

Final Note:

Does this mean that all couples who have the talk and begin to react to each other in awareness with a conscious desire for growth will find the path back to each other and have passionate sex? Of course not. Some couples will follow the path described faithfully but despite their desire to grow as individuals, they realize they have grown too far apart in the stages of their relationship prior to coming to these decisions and realizations, or perhaps even that there never was anything there to hold them together, and while they continue to further their quest for evolved partnership, it will not be with the partner with whom this process started. But this is certain: *if they have gone about the process in the way suggested in this book* (one of many possible ways, but it is the one I know), *and have truly tried to become conscious, even if they decide to separate, they will have grown immeasurably and hence the benefits of this process will be in their favor for the rest of their lives - and specifically in their partnerships - assuming they continue to live like this.*

Chapter 9

Communication: Depth Connection

Communicating With Soul

Communicating with the people who are important in our lives is something most of us do without thinking. We talk about our day at work, our colleagues, our activities, local politics, how long we had to wait in line at the supermarket, about the fact that it's time to re-negotiate the mortgage with the bank, the kids need new school uniforms, the priest/pastor/rabbi gave a great sermon last week, which movie shall we go see on the weekend, where shall we take our vacation, can we afford a vacation, June invited us to a party at her house on Saturday, my exercise class got canceled, I'm reading a new book, etc. Indeed, where would we be without real conversations with our loved ones? How can you sustain a relationship of any kind with a person you care for without communication that breaks through the barriers of social distance and gets into the parts of you that are totally real?

When an inner connection has developed between two partners (and it goes without saying that countless individuals do indeed enjoy such a connection, but this book focuses on those who are not yet there, or who may even find the whole idea of such a connection confusing), they speak their inner truth to each other and connect on deep levels through their conversations, and as already stated, the possibility for this happening presents itself when you open yourself not only to the other person, but most particularly, to your own inner truth.

Going back to the kind of things we might be talking about as described above, we could say that all of that is indeed communication, but there is very little soul in it. Well wait, you say, we also talked about my mother who needs in-home care due to her Alzheimer's, and we discussed the fact that Sinead, our middle daughter Ashley's best friend was caught taking drugs, and we're worried about Ashley running in the wrong crowd, and we discussed my growing concern about getting downsized at work.

Agreed, that is also communication, but I still contend that there is very little soul in it. All these matters are important, and clearly need to be discussed in a partnership or marriage, but most of them are, you might say, *practical* matters.

Literally we might infer that communication with depth connection implies two *souls* communicating on a soul level, as opposed to two humans communicating on a human level. But that doesn't necessarily imply talking about spiritual matters. It does, however, imply *talking about matters spiritually.* And that simply means talking with conscious awareness of yourself and of your partner (or parent, child, or friend), as well as this love that exists between the two of you, instead of talking unconsciously. This brings connection. This brings depth. This brings soul. This unites. And this allows both to grow.

And so perhaps we'll discuss how I feel about mother needing in-home care. It's brought up memories of guilt I thought I had long buried about not being a good daughter, and now the fact that a stranger might be taking care of her, has made them resurface with a vengeance. Perhaps we discuss our worries about our daughter in the light of how we lived ourselves as teens and young adults, partaking freely in recreational drugs, even though we stopped it long ago, and are now realizing the fears our parents must have had about us, and perhaps in this conversation we recognize we need to have an open talk with our daughter about the topic, and we begin to discuss how best to go about it, and how we want to deal with her from now on, perhaps in a more open way, where we are prepared for her to see that we made mistakes of the kind we fear she may now be on the verge of making, and where we risk that she may view us with new eyes on receiving this information from us. Perhaps we discuss my feelings of impotence and fear about being downsized, and perhaps that takes us to a conversation about my dreams, my aspirations, that I had never shared with you before, that have to do with making a living doing something totally unrelated to my current profession. Perhaps in this conversation I realize that you are willing to take that risk with me, for me to re-engineer my career because you care so much about me dedicating my life to something that gives great meaning to my life.

What has been so different about these conversations from the earlier examples above? In part it has to do with our mutual opening up to our *feelings,* feelings that might leave us more exposed and vulnerable to our partner, but in part it has to do with the fact that precisely those feelings create a greater soul connection between us as we talk. Further, it leads us more deeply into our own self, all the while connecting us to our partner. And it is this soul connection that gives us a firm foundation upon which to base our relationship when the going gets rough (as it does in most partnerships), without which we might not get over the hurdles.

Communicating with soul and from the position of inner truth can be cast aside, waylaid, or forgotten about so easily, as we get caught up with the practical dimension of our lives, and further, by not practicing it, we are not particularly good at it; we may even feel uncomfortable when we try to do it with our partner, our parents, and children, and even with our close friends. So making the effort to speak with soul, to find the soul and the inner truth in our communication, we are creating a depth of relationship and understanding that is not possible to achieve the other way. Oh, and there is an added benefit as we've already discussed in this book: when soul is strong in relationship, sex tends to get better and better, as opposed to getting boring and so frequently eventually becoming non-existent.

Being in Love and Loving

Let's examine once again how we love. Because *how* we love plays a massive and vitally important role in how we communicate. Love is such a vast part of life, whether because it brings sheer joy such as almost nothing else is capable of doing, or because ultimately it may lead to agonizing suffering (more often than not it is the harbinger of a bit of both). It seems quite absurd to ask if you are "in love", or if you love, since one appears to automatically imply the other. Or does it?

Being in love brings to mind that heart-pounding, mind-jolting passion we feel when the person we say we are in love with enters the room, touches us, or unexpectedly smiles or looks at us. It refers to the moments when we feel most alive, when we cannot imagine what life would be like without the other, when we most fear being abandoned by the other, when we are capable of surviving on two hours' sleep, need little food, and no matter what else occurs in our existence, we gaze benignly on life, because we are in love. The sun shines brilliantly in an impossibly azure-blue sky, even in fog, wind, rain, and storms. We pity ordinary mortals who do not share in our sublime experience, and in the rosy haze of our over-powering state of being in love we fail to see those small or large shortcomings in the beloved that are clearly and utterly obvious to others - because we are in love. Being in love – and being reciprocated in the feeling - is nearly unequalled by any other experience in life.

Loving, on the other hand rarely goes about doing so by wearing rose-colored spectacles. Loving may have begun by the less conscious state of being in love, but loving implies – you guessed it – consciousness and awareness of the reality of the other. That, in turn, implies being very aware of yourself, your thoughts, feelings, actions, and reactions. And this self awareness implies an individual who strives to take total responsibility for him or herself, who is not with another person because he or she *needs* the other person, but because the two people, by loving one another, *complement* one another from a position of individual freedom and strength. Loving is a state of affairs that is as different from being in love as day is to night. Loving, if it really *is* loving, is so much more awe-inspiring and endlessly magnificent than being in love.

So what is the difference? Imagine the pleasure you feel as a light summer breeze touches your skin. Now imagine your most mind-blowing orgasm. Imagine the satisfaction you feel after you have tidied up your office or your home after having procrastinated about it for days. Now imagine the satisfaction you feel after having released your first hit single. Imagine the happiness you feel when a puppy cuddles on your lap. Now imagine the indescribable happiness you feel when you hold your newborn in your arms the first time. I leave it up to you to guess which of each of these extremes in each sentence pair is an analogy for being in love and which is an analogy for loving.

And again, as I've inferred throughout this book, being in love makes it sound as though sex is a lot more passionate and fun than the kind of sex you might get when you love. Somehow loving seems more laid back, less erotic, less ardent, some readers may be saying. *Nothing could be further from the truth.* The consciousness factor; in other words, being aware not only of yourself but of the other in this very aware way is what makes a relationship of love (as opposed to a relationship of being in love) so extraordinarily more passionate, more erotic, and more sexually stimulating in the long term, rather than the typical short term crazy passion most of us have experienced when we are in love. Truly *knowing* the other makes the difference. Truly *seeing* the other makes the difference. Truly *loving* the other the way he or she really is, rather than the way you want or need them to be makes the difference. Obviously this implies being loved back in the same way. Having a loving relationship between two people who know themselves as they truly are makes the difference. And truly not *needing* the other for one's own well-being, and therefore being with the other out of pure love and complementarity rather than need makes the difference. Being in love implies dependence on the other for sustenance; in loving there is independence and freedom, with the simultaneous desire to be and share with the other.

So how do we get there? Clearly almost everyone starts on the "being in love" side of the coin as we have seen. Hardly anyone is conscious in the way described above, at the beginning of a relationship. Getting to the other side of the coin basically requires an understanding that the two kinds of love do exist, that the one implies dependence and the other freedom, and above all, it requires a desire to become aware and conscious of the self and of the other. I know, I know - easier said than done. But you see, once you know that this is what it requires, you can never go back to the old way of thinking without deceiving yourself. So now you have a choice to make, and by making it, you have the power to begin to change all your relationships.

* * * * * * * * * * * * * * *

But first, of course, long before we reach the place where we have the awareness to be able to consciously choose to have the power to change our relationships, things happen. It starts gradually, as time passes. You realize, one day, that although there is still love, there is no real connection anymore between the two of you. Perhaps you realize it suddenly, and perhaps what you realize – even while you acknowledge that there is still love - is not that there is no real connection anymore, *but that there never was one.*

Most people look for connection with their partner by the mere virtue of the fact that they are "in love". Beyond that, perhaps they have tried to choose a partner from a similar social environment, or someone with similar intellectual and educational requisites. Interests, hobbies, professional and social aims and personal goals in life may be of prime importance, as is the desire to form a family, educate the ensuing children within a particular religion or philosophy, and so on. Evidently a good sexual connection tends to be of high importance for the majority of individuals as well.

The subject here is *not* whether the couple no longer even likes each other, or one of the two has found a new partner outside of the relationship, or finds the other partner hateful, boring, disgusting, or any number of other equally negative adjectives. Quite the contrary, in the situation I am describing, the partners continue to harbor loving feelings for one another. So: what changes?

As the years go by, it is possible that hobbies and general interests change in one or the other of the partners, that sexuality wanes, that even goals and aims in life have begun to shift due to any number of events that may have occurred over the years and affected one or both partners in a myriad number of ways.

The children are now no longer dreams in their parents' minds, nor are they adorable babies, but may be teenagers, and may appear to have become members of an alien race (for a time), and may have caused further distances between the parents as they struggle to understand how best to be parents to these difficult people in that in-between stage we call the *Sturm und Drang* of adolescence.

But the loss of clarity of all or some of these elements is not what I am referring to when I address the topic of *connection*. A "real" connection in a love relationship goes far beyond the basic attractor factors that pull us to other people. These serve to do that initial job of getting us together. The chemistry, the physical attraction, the conversations that show us that this person is on the same page as we are (or not, as the case may be, but perhaps because they are *not*, we are even more attracted), the *desirability* of precisely that person within the parameters of our particular "world", are merely some of the mechanisms that help us understand – in hindsight – the reasons we actually desired a union with a specific individual. But these still tell us nothing of the real connection.

The real connection has to do with our inner self. It has to do with our inner energy and, as David Hawkins, author of *Power vs Force* would put it, our inner power. In other words, the real connection has to come from a place where that which an individual truly is, on a level that goes far beyond the everyday mundane human things we all do in life, connects him or her to the partner's same inner self.

That's rather a mouthful. What you may be starting to get a glimpse of here, is the fact that this inner self is the part of you that you can only get to know if you decide to get to know yourself. Not necessarily by going into therapy or counseling, but simply by taking that most sacred and *necessary* journey into yourself, looking at yourself with total honesty, in order to begin to understand not only *why* you are as you are, but also *what you can truly make of yourself* in the greater scheme of things.

Such an inner knowing, which unfortunately most people tend not to spend too much time on, due to the fact that in our culture such a quest is given far less importance than the quest for socio-economic abundance and prestige (also very important, but the inner quest should at least be on the same level as the outer one), brings us to a place where the type of connection we can form with others goes far beyond the more mundane and practical connections referred to earlier.

Such a connection to the self – due to the importance an individual places on the inner knowing, or the inner quest, brings about the possibility of attracting people into one's life that are on a similar search.

But what happens when someone who has not given this much thought, reaches the point described earlier, and realizes that although there may still be love, there is not, in fact, a real connection with the partner? And believes, furthermore, that because there is no real connection, there is no longer much of anything holding the relationship together, which generally means that sex has also loosened its hold and is no longer very attractive for one or both of the partners.

If this couple could come to understand that what has been lost (or what never was), is *not the change of goals and aims, or the change of interests in life, or the difficulty with the children*, but the fact that neither of the two ever developed their *own* connection to their inner self. *Without such a connection, the outer, energetic (which also means "sexual", among many other things) connection to the partner can never be as strong, as with it.* With such a connection, the "spark", that so many people feel was lost after the honeymoon remains strong – *and continually grows* - throughout the lifetime of both partners. Just think what a difference that would make!

So what can you do? First of all, it's never too late to start. Any time is a good time, the main thing is, that you start. It's akin to waking up from a deep sleep. The more you wake up, the more you begin to take in. Secondly, the "how" to start varies greatly. You might delve more deeply into the subject by reading more extensively about it. You might attend seminars, or view some online clips. You might begin practicing gratitude, mindfulness or begin to meditate (also see the Appendix). Or you might follow an intuition you have had, that has nothing to do with any of the above, but simply *speaks to you* and you know that if you follow it, it might let you see something important more clearly. You can read many of the transpersonal, spiritual, and integral authors available to all of us. Much is even freely (and legally) available on the web in the form of e-book, video, or audio clip downloads (see the Appendix for some suggestions). You might decide to first have an all-important talk with your partner in order to explain that you want to venture out on the as yet unexplored path of self-discovery, but you would really like to do so together. And the connection you seek may begin to flourish more quickly than you could imagine.

Recognizing Yourself in the Mirror of the Beloved

When you see your own reflection in the mirror of your relationships by virtue of *your reactions to others,* you hold the magic wand that can help you begin to understand yourself in your own hands. What can and should you do when faced with your reactions to others in your life?

The underlying structure to my answer lies in the Socratic advice: *Physician, know thyself.* In other words, it is necessary to begin *the process of knowing yourself and recognizing your own issues.* In such a case, when faced with an individual you may hypothetically not like, you would understand that the reason you feel unpleasant in the presence of that person has nothing in particular to do with him or her, *but with you.*

That of course signifies that you can't blame that person for how you feel. (Please note, right now I'm not talking about your relationships, simply about someone you might have met at a social event and you noticed that something about that person was not agreeable to you.)

So: no blaming. Even if the person is obnoxious, or difficult, or needy, or haughty, or self-serving, or autocratic, judgmental, querulous, or self-pitying, or whatever it might be *that sets you off.* What sets you off is not his/her behavior, *but some unresolved issue in you.* Here is why: if the issue were resolved in you, *it would not set you off.* Affect (emotion) is an immense and very helpful clue to something that needs addressing in oneself. So that means you're the one that has to look at yourself, i.e., it's not a question of looking outward and pointing a finger. (Again, please note, it is very possible that the other person is indeed very obnoxious or unpleasant, but that is not what concerns us. What concerns us your reaction to it. It simply would not bother you if your own inner issues had been resolved. You would be able to overlook it, or to not let it bother you. Something about that person's behavior sets off your issues.)

Jewels in Our Lives

So back to the hypothetical person you don't like. *Such an individual could well become a jewel in your life,* if you're willing to follow the above directive of knowing yourself and if you're willing to look within, rather than without. So such a person - assuming you have reached a certain level of awareness in your life - immediately sets off a warning bell, and launches a red flag in you, to make you aware of the fact that this particular person is bringing out some as yet unresolved issue.

The example I've used is someone you met at a social event, not a partner, but this is how it is *with every single person that populates your life*, from the peripheral fringes, to its nuclear core, from the newspaper vendor and shoeshine person, to your partner and children or parents. Every time you react on the inside to something or someone, you are being given a message about yourself by your psyche, and if you pay close (and loving) attention to those messages, if you look into your own reflection in the mirror of your relationship with that particular person, you will learn something about yourself, and eventually have the possibility to resolve that issue in order to not have to revisit that place again, in such a way that *similar situations in future, will not affect you negatively* as they used to do. And so you begin to connect to yourself in completely new ways.

Evidently none of this is of no use whatsoever to you if you do not apply this new-found or new-recognized knowledge about yourself in the way in which you now communicate with your partner. How you now react *must* take this new awareness into consideration. You can no longer just react. You begin to connect on another level.

Communicating and Remaining Conscious

Clearly in order to communicate at the level this chapter has been examining, it is imperative that you remain conscious. If you slip into blind reactivity as we have already discussed at length, you have no chance at achieving either your own transformation, nor that of your partnership, nor of allowing your partner to see this new you that comes from a position of recognition and understanding that relationship issues are in fact, gifts for each partner's own psycho-emotional and spiritual growth and evolution. But what *is being* conscious? What does it mean when we are *not* conscious? *Why* are we not conscious? And *how* can we remain conscious?

Over the millennia being conscious has been defined in many ways by scores of seekers, masters, enlightened beings, philosophers and spiritual or mystical organizations, as well as countless spiritual authors:

- It has been defined as: subjectivity, awareness, the ability to experience or to feel, wakefulness, having a sense of selfhood
- John Locke (1690) defined it as *the perception of what passes in a man's own mind*
- Stuart Sutherland (1989) wrote in the *MacMillan Dictionary of Psychology* about being conscious: *The having of perceptions, thoughts, and feelings; awareness. The term is impossible to define except in terms that are unintelligible without a grasp of what consciousness means. Many fall into the trap of equating consciousness with self-consciousness—to be conscious it is only necessary to be aware of the external world. Consciousness is a fascinating but elusive phenomenon: it is impossible to specify what it is, what it does, or why it has evolved*
- Some seek to define it in purely Newtonian and mechanistic terms, i.e. that it all comes down to something physical or tangible
- The mystical psychiatrist Richard Maurice Bucke distinguished between three types of consciousness: *Simple Consciousness*, awareness of the body, possessed by many

animals; *Self Consciousness*, awareness of being aware, possessed only by humans; and *Cosmic Consciousness*, awareness of the life and order of the universe, possessed only by humans who are enlightened

- Ken Wilber described consciousness as a spectrum with ordinary awareness at one end, and more profound types of awareness at higher levels

- Carl Gustav Jung said it involved bringing aspects of the collective unconscious (a part of the collective mind, shared by all people and all of humankind) *into awareness* and then becoming more aware of the workings of your own psyche and the meaning of individuation, or becoming more what you really are.

So to simplify and for the purposes of this discussion, we could say that being conscious implies being aware of the self at all times, or at the very least, intending and attempting to be aware of the self, in such a way that no matter what occurs, this awareness is never lost in the waves of events over the course of an hour, a day, or a lifetime. On another scale, being conscious also implies an acute awareness of a self that goes beyond the physical body with which we are clothed - an awareness of an eternal self that does not cease to exist when the body does. On an even deeper level, being conscious signifies knowing and recognizing the divinity of the self *and* that same divinity in *everyone* with whom we are all, furthermore, energetically connected.

Evidently it follows that when you are not conscious you are not aware of yourself. You might notice - be conscious of - getting sick, although something like a back ache or a stiff neck might not make itself noticeable for a while either, simply because you would have less awareness about your physical self as well. You might not notice something like a gut feeling, an intuition, or even if you did, your awareness of it might be so reduced, that you simply would not pay attention to it.

On another level, you would not notice your SELF in daily interaction with others. You would notice the things they said or did to you, but you would yet not have sufficient awareness or consciousness to be able to observe your own inner reactions to that, *in order to then be able to choose other, perhaps less toxic reactions* because that kind of *choice* is only possible when you are fully conscious.

You would not notice your *egoic self* (we might describe that as the part of you that sees everything *first and foremost* from its own point of view) *intruding* in everyday activities when, for example, you might be insisting on being right, whether or not you were, and even if you were, despite the fact that going to those lengths to show that you were right, might break a particular relationship asunder, or at least, damage it, as in the kind of damage vested upon relationships with our partners and children in such situations, your egoic self would make you *insist on showing you were right*.

You simply might *not hear* something kind your partner, parent or child just said, because closely attached (in verbal distance) to the kind words, were *other* words your mind has latched upon that you now interpret as being critical, harsh or cruel, and *even if they were*, the fact is, that due to a lack of full awareness or consciousness, you have merely heard and reacted to the more negative words.

Not being conscious has ramifications that spread themselves like grasping, strangling tentacles into every sector of our lives, literally cutting off the oxygen that allows us to live a healthy existence filled with inner freedom and well-being. Being partially conscious is helpful but not nearly enough.

Why are we not conscious? There are a number of quite logical answers to this question:

- We may not be aware of another kind of existence other than our 'sleeping' one
- We may be aware, but have not yet taken any kind of decision to become more conscious
- We may be aware, but do not desire to take any kind of decision to become more conscious
- We may have taken the decision, but do not follow through on it with practice and discipline and a continual reminding of ourselves
- We may have taken the decision, and are even following through on it, but only to a degree, and hence, despite our best intentions – simply because we are still too *weak* in

that arena – continually forget to *practice* remaining conscious

How can we remain conscious? Remaining conscious involves intent, choice and practice.

Intent means that your *intention* is to remain conscious. If you intend to lose weight, you will be paying attention to a number of things such as the kind of food you have in your house, the amount of food you have on your plate, and all the food choices you make throughout your day *every* day.

Intending to remain conscious works in a similar fashion. You *pay attention* to things such as your body and how it reacts, your emotions and how they are reacting, thoughts, and your inner energy and the level it is at.

Choice means that you *choose* to remain conscious. If you choose to lose weight, you will choose to purchase certain foods and not others, you will choose to eat certain foods in public places and not others, and you will choose to say no to unhealthy food choices when someone offers them to you.

Choosing to remain conscious works in a similar fashion. You *choose* to do certain things that will promote remaining conscious. You may do some mindfulness exercises, such as a 15-minute mindfulness walk every day* that will promote the growth of new neural pathways that will literally help you remain conscious and in a state of inner balance and well-being.

Practice means that you *practice* remaining conscious. If you practice losing weight, you will attune your body to a new way of eating, because you are using this new way over and over until it becomes a habit.

Practicing to remain conscious works in a similar fashion. You *practice* certain activities and new thought patterns because you know full well that what is not practiced does not become a habit, and if it does not become a habit, nothing will change.

Remaining conscious is truly a full-time activity, although it does not actually take much time. It takes a habit of mindfulness, expressed in your daily intent, your daily choices, and what you practice on a daily basis.

*15-Minute Mindfulness Walk: choose a time, during daylight hours when you can walk unimpeded, on your own, for 15 minutes. Start by focusing on the beauty around you, whether this is beauty you see, smell, hear, taste or touch. When you do this, also allow yourself to feel gratitude for whatever it is you are perceiving with one or more of your senses. This brings you into the present moment, allowing your mind to be still. Notice the sensation - albeit brief - of momentary peace. Then do it again, by noticing something else, and again, feel the gratitude and again notice the inner peace. Try to continue doing this for the entire 15 minutes. If at one point you realize your thoughts have wandered off to your worries or past pain, or just everyday problems, don't get annoyed with yourself. Simply pull yourself back to noticing beauty again until your 15 minutes are up.

****

Communication that springs from a well of conscious awareness on both sides, communication that is transparent, and communication that seeks to further the spiritual evolution of both partners, is a depth connection that is most often not present in our relationships. Achieving this kind of depth connection is not impossible, but it does require intention and attention, recognition and awareness, and at least as much love for the self as there is for the partner.

Chapter 10

Recognizing That THIS
Is How Growth Takes Place

Occasionally the process of growth begins because we fall in love with what I am choosing to call the *wrong person* - perhaps more than once. This is not because the person is, in fact, wrong, but because without awareness, that is how it appears to us initially when we begin to experience problems in the relationship.

We've all known people of whom we say: *how on earth were they ever attracted to each other? They are so different!* Such a couple may remain together through thick and thin even though they have challenges, or, conversely, they may split up quite quickly after the initial honeymoon stage. But *what* is it that happens, and more importantly, *why* does it happen?

Let's examine a few cases:

- Stavros and Eleni had been to school together decades earlier in their native Greece. She had moved to California immediately after finishing her education and had started an import-export business of high-grade copies of Greek artifacts. Stavros remained in Greece and pursued his career. Both married. He more than once. She became successful. He didn't. They lost contact. Until one fateful day in Athens. She had gone back for some business meetings and went to a dinner and who was there but Stavros. They quickly resumed talking as though they had seen each other the day before. The *frisson* was there, it just felt right, and so he came to visit her in California, and soon they had agreed that it might be a good idea if he moved there to help her with her business. Eventually they married. He signed a pre-nup. All seemed rosy. But then it started falling apart. She lost her patience at his lack of business acumen and let him know it - frequently. He lost his patience with her aging process and was outrageously flirtatious in their (i.e., *her*) social circle. Both began to drink more. Communication - *real* communication, if that ever even existed - was no longer taking place. Blame became the name of the game. And so they divorced.

- Sabine and Tristan met at a pub. Classical story about a boy from a good family, and a girl from a more simple family. They were only six months apart in age, but she behaved like a clucking mother hen around him. She was the first girl he ever had sex with. She got pregnant. Mainly due to his social circle, they decided to marry. His interests were wide-flung and as varied as the colors of the rainbow; hers were narrow and grey. And so they began to grow apart before they had even found themselves, and eventually he asked for a divorce in order to remove himself from the stifling and suffocating atmosphere of her lackluster mind and disapproval of his *joie de vivre*.

- Richard and Christina met at a gym in a small town in Iowa. She was a client and he was a personal trainer. She came from a socially and academically strong background; his family was poor and he never finished high school. Nevertheless, despite her background, she lacked self-esteem, and he did as well, but to an even greater degree. She found it very hard to socialize normally, but felt good with him in the gym and due to this good feeling around him, so different from the awkward feelings she generally had around others, she fell in love with him. She began spending much more time at the gym, recognizing that little connected them other than her training and her feelings, but *craving* those feelings. He, of course, was flattered that she was so interested in him, and also fell in love with her. Under the circumstance you might think it could work. Whether it will or not, remains to be seen. But you will agree, I believe, that they are two opposites, and that at first glance, it's a relationship that makes little sense. *Why do they appear to need each other?*

- Siobhan and Christian met on a skiing trip at a high-end resort in France. She was recently divorced, sophisticated, beautiful and seeking her next well-heeled partner. He was intellectual and sporty, but sophistication was not in his vocabulary. In fact, and despite his healthy bank account, he was rather needy. And so he fell for the sensuality of her enchantment in a big way. By so doing, the luster she had initially seen when contemplating him as a potential mate, became rather tarnished. He was - in her eyes - no longer as desirable due to his overt need for her, and so, in her quest for a stronger mate, she had a blatant and highly public affair that broke his heart.

- Roger and Gwyneth met online in his native London. They both had impressive academic degrees: he was a thoracic surgeon and she was an IT specialist for a large multinational corporation. He was Jewish and she was Catholic but neither cared about that, especially once she decided to convert. He was fifteen years her senior, both had been previously married, and both had children from their prior relationships. They also had another child together. They were well-suited intellectually. Both had been very hurt in those prior marriages. Their emotions were in some fashion stunted, and so in that sense, they meshed well, since neither required a great deal of emotional expression from the other. Their respective feelings of pain and fear were stuffed down into psychic netherworlds that neither was keen on exploring. So what went wrong?

Each of these vignettes depicts a relationship that often makes - for the outsider who views it dispassionately - little sense. And yet in each case, at least on the side of one of the partners, if not both, something arose that was perceived as true love. So why do we so often - apparently - fall in love with the "wrong" person?

Projection, as we have seen, is part of it. What we are *not* - or what is *missing* in us - if we can see that piece which is missing in us in the other, is often what we fall in love with. In a way, it's like falling in love with yourself, because if you can see it in the other, and love it, it means that in some fashion it also exists in you, albeit in the nascent, as yet not developed and exteriorized state. (And as a side note, what you fall in love with in the other, is always worthy of examination for greater self-understanding because it speaks of a part that belongs to you that you have *not yet recognized as being yours*). Note: the piece that is missing in us is not generally something we are aware of. Hence the projection. *We only see it in the other.*

Another part of falling in love with the "wrong" person, as we have also discussed, is need. Which is tantamount to saying projection and need are strongly intertwined. If I love what is in you - or better said - if I fall in love with what I perceive as being in you, but it's actually part of me (see previous paragraph), then by loving it in *you*, I am loving *myself*. So while I am with you, I am able to love myself. But if you leave, if our relationship fails, I feel devastated - in part because I am no longer able to love myself (the part of me that I perceive in you that I fell in love with). Therefore, I *need you in order to be able to love myself.*

So those two factors alone are enormous problems in our relationships.

Let's take the projection/need dyad one step further. Instead of leaving me, you began showing me other aspects of your personality that mean that I am no longer able to *see* the parts that I fell in love with. I blame you of course, because you *changed*. But what is really happening under the surface, is that due to what I perceive as change in you, and no longer being able to see the parts

I fell in love with, I am no longer able to love *myself*. I feel cheated, betrayed, bereft, I may even feel physically nauseous, and the last place I would consider looking in order to resolve this dilemma, is at myself!

Assuming you are still with me and assuming you are giving this information the benefit of the doubt, you may ask: *but what is it all for*? That, I believe, is the most important question because it leads to an answer that brings us much more information than the first question. As we have seen over and over again in this book, difficulty in relationships serves a very important purpose in our quest for growth (always assuming we are interested in such a phenomenon), because it is in the unraveling of the projection / need dyad that we begin to see ourselves and understand ourselves in ways that were not clear before.

If we follow this Ariadne's thread into the self by way of relationship, we furthermore have the opportunity of moving from mere relationship into spiritual partnership, where we become very aware of the opportunities that the kind of love that comes from two individuals who love each other freely and independently offers us, as opposed to the needy and dependent kind of love we find before we become conscious.

It can all happen in the same relationship - this move from relationship to spiritual partnership - but it requires coming to consciousness. And that process requires accepting that there is always a choice, assuming responsibility for the self, and learning to love the self.

Listening to the Gut: Boundaries & Self-Love

On other occasions the process of growth begins because we start - finally - to listen to our *gut*, to our intuition which often initiates the recognition of our unhealthy boundaries and lack of self-love.

Imagine I were one of your best friends. I give you a call and tell you that I'm going through a rather rough patch and need to talk to someone. And I tell you that you are such a good listener and that you give great advice. So could we please have dinner tomorrow night? As it happens, you have some rather fun plans for tomorrow. However, because I am your good friend, you agree to break those plans and see me. You suggest we meet at a restaurant we've been at together in the past at 8:30 pm the following evening.

The next day, at about six, I call you, and tell you that I just ran into Robert, and I remind you about how much I have always been attracted to him, and that he has invited me out to dinner tonight. I say: *You don't mind, do you*?

Now your mind is churning with thoughts. *WHAT???* you think, *Yesterday you were falling apart and needed to speak to someone and so asked me for time, and you know I broke my own plans to accommodate you, and now you are blowing me off*? But, as you are thinking these thoughts, you are also remembering that I am your very good friend, and so now, the question is: *how do you react to what I have just said to you*?

Let me interrupt here and explain that this hypothetical situation is one that I often pose to clients. I need to know what their reaction would be in this kind of a situation that happens - as I am confident you will agree - rather more frequently than we might like.

So: *how do you react to my announcement that I am going to dinner with Robert and not with you*?

(Please do think of your response - or remember the last time you were in a similar situation and how you reacted then - before reading on).

Here's the thing: many, many people respond that while they don't like it, they do in fact say that it's ok and that the other person may go ahead and have dinner with Robert.

So if this had been a test, those of you who answered the way many do, let me assure you that you failed miserably. But the reason you failed has to do with the fact that you have let *yourself* down.

Whenever I pose this hypothetical scenario, I then ask the client: *do you not notice that when you are being blown off, and when you allow it, by not saying anything about it, that your gut clenches painfully*? And again, most will tell me - and I am confident that in your case it is also the same - that it does indeed clench painfully. And they will often tell me that this clenching is a *well-known* feeling.

Let me tell you that this clenching is a message from your body to you. We can also call it intuition, although of course intuition may come as well in the guise of thoughts that we pay scant attention to. But what I can guarantee is this: if you do indeed begin to pay attention to signs you receive from your body, you will also begin to pay much greater attention to other kinds of intuitive knowing. What the clenching is saying is that you need to address this situation. You need to say to the other person that what he/she is doing is not acceptable.

So *if you do not want to let yourself down*, it is imperative that you learn how to react in situations where others do or say something that you find unacceptable, and that you understand what their different reactions to you (assuming you now let them know you find it unacceptable) may mean as well. *This forms part of learning how to love yourself.*

First of all: when you feel the clenching, take it to be a message from yourself through that second brain you have in your gut (for more information about our second and third brains, please see *Rewiring the Soul*), that it is absolutely essential that you do something about it. As stated earlier, if you do nothing when you have that very physical feeling, you are letting yourself down. It is tantamount to saying to yourself on this subliminal level, that you are not worth it; that you do not respect yourself enough to do it, and more importantly, that you do not love yourself enough to do it. *What do you think a lifetime of giving yourself that message, does to you*?

Once you have recognized that something needs to be done, understand that this something is based *not* on you correcting the other person, or becoming angry at the other person, or showing the other person how horrible they are, or how inconsiderate, or changing their way of being; rather, is based *on you seeing that you care enough about yourself to speak up when an unacceptable thing is being done or said to you.* (Please note that if this is a case of domestic violence, this method should not be used).

This means that by speaking up about yourself, you will automatically *feel better* about yourself! You literally empower yourself because you are beginning the process of setting up healthy boundaries. The clenching in your gut was *speaking* to you about your *unhealthy* boundaries and your lack of self-love indicating that you would be well-advised to do something about both.

So if you need to speak up without getting angry, it follows that whatever you *do* say, needs to come from a place of calmness (even though when you begin to do this, your heart will beat in a most frightful fashion, because you will not be accustomed to doing this, and it will provoke a fear of rejection from the other in you). From this place of calmness, you can say something along the lines that whatever was just said or done is not acceptable, that it is hurtful, or inconsiderate, and in the example offered above, it shows you that the other person (who is standing you up), does not value your friendship the same way you do. You also need to give a consequence (albeit a small one since is the first time you are speaking up about the matter at hand with this particular person), so you might simply say: *Please don't do it again.* It's not actually a consequence, but you *are* putting the other person on guard with respect to a repetition of their behavior.

When I explain this to clients, the reaction is frequently one of tension: *no*, they say**,** *I could never do that. I could not say such words to another person.* Then, of course, when I mention that the reason they feel they can't, is because they fear the other's reaction of potential rejection, I point out that this is a long-ingrained habit (probably rooted in childhood, although not necessarily due to abusive behavior as much as due to perceived reactions on the part of your parents or caretakers) of allowing others to step on them in unacceptable ways (or of allowing boundaries to be trespassed in order to be approved of by pleasing the other, or simply by not annoying the other by speaking up), that is literally eating away at them, and it needs to be conquered in order that they may begin to feel some love for themselves. Conquering it - as conquering anything at all - is a question of tiny step after tiny step. Practice plus intention plus conscious choice will take you there.

Having now imagined that this was indeed braved, and said, I then offer several possible reactions on the part of the other. One, of course, is the dreaded rejection, where the 'friend' generally says something in a rather loud, belligerent or offensive tone of voice to the tune of: *what is wrong with you, it's just a dinner, I don't see what you are getting yourself so worked up about*, and in the meantime you are shriveling up inside because - just as you feared - you are being rejected.

At this point, I then ask the client: *And is this really the kind of friend you want*? This bears some thinking about. And remember, the friend is reacting this way in part because he/she is used to you allowing them to step all over you. *You have accustomed them to such behavior. Perhaps the matter is worth discussing in the not-too-distant future with this person, if you are interested in moving the friendship into better avenues.*

However, let's assume the other person had a better reaction, and - hand over mouth - says something like: *Oh, I am so sorry! I don't know what I was thinking. Let me re-arrange matters and let's have dinner after all.* Clearly this is another kettle of fish, and not only are you feeling better now because you spoke up, but more importantly, because something has been cleared up between the two of you, perhaps after decades of 'unacceptable' behavior on the part of your friend and mute acceptance on your part, and so you can both move forward on a new basis. Further, you have learned that this person is a true friend indeed.

Sadly, as you can imagine, the former reaction is much more typical, at which point your conversation has probably ended. However, despite all this, it may happen that you nevertheless continue in contact with this person, and some months down the road a similar situation ensues. At this point, you really need to refer to the first time you brought it up: *we already had a situation like this a couple of months ago, and I asked you not to repeat it. You clearly respect our friendship much less than I do, so I am going to think about this whole thing. I'll be in touch when I've reached a conclusion.* Once again, you are affirming to yourself that you care enough about yourself to do this, and you are showing the other person, not only that it is indeed unacceptable to treat you this way, but you are now putting a concrete consequence into the equation: don't call me, I'll call you ... once I've thought about this.

This entire situation (illustrated with one very tiny example, and of course other examples abound in the lives of those who do not take on the responsibility of proving to themselves that they love themselves) and your new behavior will bring you closer to yourself, to an inner connection to yourself and in this process you will be showing yourself that you are on the path to loving yourself in a new and much more healthy way. *This is one of the roads to the necessary growth required for healthy spiritual partnerships and to inner freedom and well-being.*

Messages From the Body

Let's examine those messages your body sends you a bit more closely, because although we have already had a look at them, their purpose in our process of growth is undeniable. You might think of them as emails coming to you from your body. Our bodies offer us information all the time. Such as: I stubbed my toe (*walk more carefully*), or I burned my finger (*light the candles with a longer match*), or I'm out of breath (*walk a bit more slowly*), or my head hurts (*put on those sunglasses*), or I've got a toothache (*go to the dentist and stop eating so many sweets*).

We all know those messages from our body, and tend to pay attention to them, because a direct physical consequence - something that is making us uncomfortable - results if we don't take care of the message.

And yet, our bodies, in their infinite wisdom, send us so many more messages that are potentially far more important, with much greater consequences, that we frequently pay scant attention to.

Check out these examples (the words in parentheses are merely possibilities - under no circumstances am I saying that these are *always* underlying the symptom):

- stiff neck (tension, anger, inflexibility)
- aching lower back (stress, worry, fear)
- headache (stress, worry, heart pain, fear)
- burning sensation in the gut (anger, stress, resentment)
- high blood pressure (stress, tension, underlying overwork)
- constipation (unhealthy life style on many levels, and also inflexibility)
- lack of enthusiasm, lack of physical energy (unhealthy life style - on many levels, for example, poor boundaries)
- insomnia (worry, stress, emotional pain, anger, etc.)

In all of these examples (and many more I have not enumerated), of course we tend to do something about the symptom, we may make an appointment to see a doctor, or a chiropractor, or physiotherapist, etc., but we *tend not to do anything about the underlying causes*, most often because we are not aware of them because this is not a language in which we are schooled.

We pay no attention to the email we've just received from our body. And the email we receive from our body in this way, is similar to the first letter the bank writes you, when you are late in paying the mortgage. They are encouraging you to look for a solution. But if you pay no attention, more letters will follow, each one with a darker underlying message, until finally, if you are still not doing anything about it, you lose your house.

Our bodies are wise - sometimes I think they are so much wiser than we are despite all of the use we give our so-called rational brain. So the wisdom of our bodies sends us these little messages *that we are meant to pay attention to.* Our bodies are giving us information *in plenty of time*, so that we can change something about the way we go about our lives, so that we can change something about the way we deal with our emotions, in order that we can *catch the problem long before it becomes dangerous.*

But what do we do? We tend to try to fix the outer symptom, without looking at the underlying causes. If there is a crack in a major holding wall in my house, it is possible that the problem is only in the wall. But it is also possible that the problem is structural in a much more important way than the mere observation of the crack might tell us.

And so it is with our bodies. Think of the number of times you have heard of studies that indicate that people who have died of heart problems often had difficulties related to love and emotions in their lives. Perhaps they experienced a complicated situation with the partner, the family, with the children, and so on. We could literally say that *their heart was broken*. Or how about the number of times we have all read about the fact that cancer begins with stress. Hello? Stress? Yes - just look at some of the studies that psycho-neuro-immunology (PNI) has come up with about this subject - and remember that emotional pain of the type that causes bitterness and resentment also has been shown to bring on many different kinds of cancer.

Can you imagine that heart burn might not only have to do with having eaten something that does not agree with you, but also have to do with anger or emotional pain? And that if you don't decide to look at the underlying causes, and only treat the outer symptoms, it might lead you to a place where more important aspects of your health might be involved?

And heartburn is only one example. I could refer to many others, such as nausea (you might be nauseous because you spend time with a person who continually transgresses your boundaries as in the example above, or someone who frequently hurts you emotionally, perhaps by being emotionally unavailable). If these situations are not dealt with by you - perhaps by looking at yourself to determine why you allow such behavior - you may need to deal with them in a very physical way some years hence, so the little email from your body in the guise of nausea is hugely valuable and most definitely worthwhile checking out carefully.

Check your mail frequently - regard it as a gift, as you would regard mail from someone you love very much. Think of it in that way, and start paying attention to the messages. They also have the capacity to help you grow closer to the possibility of spiritual partnership.

The Different Faces of Love

Another aspect in our process towards growth is that we begin to recognize love in all of its faces. Recognizing love - and how love shows its face - applies not only to our partners or spouses, but also to other members of the extended family, and certainly also to friends.

How do we normally recognize love? People tell us that they love us. They do lovely things for us. They make us feel good. They are kind, considerate; in short, they are *loving*. And you are probably thinking: *I certainly did not need to read this in order to find that out*!

Bear with me. You know that someone loves you, i.e., you *recognize the love* because what they do *resonates* with what you consider to be loving. However, when they don't do this, or no longer do this, then you tend to consider the possibility that they do not love you.

But in the instance of them not doing things that resonate with what you consider to be loving, could it not be that the two of you simply speak different languages of what love is? And how love is represented? And how love shows its face? Take, for instance, an adult daughter who does not hug her parents very much, nor does she express her feelings for them continually, but she is constantly bringing them dishes she cooks for their freezer, so that they no longer need to cook their own meals. Or take, as another example, a friend who is always late for appointments with you, but is, in fact, the only one of your friends you can really trust to tell you the truth about yourself. What about the husband who finds it enormously hard to publicly express any kind of affection for you, and yet is always doing all in his power to ensure your comfort and material ease?

Examples abound, and the point I particularly want to get across, is the fact that *our expectations of love* do not necessarily coincide with the love we receive, and yet, if we are open to it, that does not mean that we are not receiving love, simply that we must learn to recognize it *in this other format.*

When you learn the English word for *butter*, and I am German, in which case the word is *Butter*, I easily recognize it. But then if another person learns the word in Spanish where it is *mantequilla* or in French where it is *buerre*, it may be harder to recognize for what it is. Analogically, a similar thing happens in our differing conceptions of how to show love. So let's learn to recognize that another may show as much love as we do, but in ways that are not *our* ways. That does not make it less worthy, nor does it mean we are loved in a less valuable way.

What Exactly Do We Love When We Love?

A further aspect in our process towards growth has to do with a recognition and understanding - an awareness - on our part of what we love when we love. Have you ever given it any thought? What, in fact, do we love, when we love?

- Do we love the feeling of being loved (as opposed to not feeling loved before)?
- Do we love the feeling of being adored (as opposed to not feeling adored before)?
- Do we love the feeling of being doted on (as opposed to not feeling doted on before)?
- Do we love the feeling of being important to someone (as opposed to not feeling important before)?
- Do we love feeling fulfilled (as opposed to how unfulfilled we felt before)?
- Do we love feeling secure (as opposed to how insecure we felt before)?
- Do we love feeling needed (as opposed to not feeling needed before)?
- Do we love how good we feel when we are with the other (as opposed to not feeling nearly as good without the other)?
- Do we love knowing we are not alone (as opposed to how we feel when we are alone)?
- Do we love how the other gazes into our eyes (as opposed to how we feel when no one gazes into our eyes)?
- Do we love the fact that the other appears to only have eyes for us?
- Do we love the feeling of being excluded from the world?
- Do we love how the other shows us how much we are loved?

You might say to me, but of course, all of that is normal when you are in love, and I would not disagree with you in the least. But how much of that has to do with *you*? I mean: how much of it has to do with *how* this being in love makes you feel? What have you said, or thought, about the other, with the exception of *how the other makes you feel*? Have you examined where the other is in all of this? Don't worry, I'm not implying that you are selfish.

I'm actually asking you to consider that perhaps a part of this whole business of *what we love when we love* has much more to do with satisfying a deep longing inside ourselves that we are not capable of taking care of - or so we think, or have been taught to believe - on our own. And so we *need*, so to speak, the other to take care of it for us. The other fulfills us, being with other makes us feel secure, needed, important, valuable, etc.

What is this longing? Why does the fulfilling of it by the other make us feel so good? (At least until the relationship palls or goes sour). The longing is, as I indicated earlier, for our self-love. We are not taught - generally - to love ourselves, and so *we need to fulfill that need with another.* Thus we seek to do so through our love relationships. And that is precisely why so many of them go sour.

If we could learn to fulfill our own needs in that vastly misunderstood arena of self-love, the weight of responsibility in the relationship for making us feel good about ourselves would gradually no longer need to rest on the hapless shoulders of our unwitting partner. We would assume responsibility for it ourselves. And our love relationships would be lighter (by not being burdened by such a load), and yet more profound because two individuals who come together, already having learned to fulfill their own needs, already having assumed responsibility for their own inner well-being, already having begun the road towards self-love, will reach depths of love that people involved in the other kind of relationship can only dream of.

Differentiation & Autonomy

Another aspect in our process towards growth is differentiating from our partner and finding autonomy in love. Typically when autonomy in love gets discussed in my office, people object, because we believe and we feel, that when we love, when we are in love, there is no longer any room for autonomy, as we are, so to speak, glued at the hip.

Oh, we all know that you leave in the morning to go to your office, and I go to mine, and that furthermore you have your poker night out, or perhaps it's football, or even opera, or the photography class, and I have my bridge club night out, or perhaps it's my book club night or even night classes at law school for the next who-knows-how-many years - so *of course* we aren't glued at the hip. Don't you see, we do so much apart, we even have some friends we don't share and all these activities. *Really, glued at the hip - not us*, my clients firmly tell me, *we are of another generation than our parents.*

I agree. We do all of the above and more and so *apparently* we are no longer glued at the hip the way so many previous generations were. We make our own money, our own decisions and have become quite emancipated in all matters pertaining to love, no matter our gender.

But this is what is missing, not with everyone, but with many: we continue to be glued at the hip *because we still fall apart if our partner is not in a good place with us*. By that I mean that if you see his/her face over the breakfast table looking at you in a certain way, or if he/she comes home from work with that look on his/her face, you already know something is wrong and *it affects you in your innermost self, in that place where you feel good or bad about yourself*, even if your partners swears it has nothing to do with you.

In a nutshell, what is happening is that your well-being is hung up inside the place where you feel good only as long as the beloved is also in a good place. When he/she is not, due to any number of reasons external to the relationship, and is not in a good place him or herself, then you find it very difficult to extricate yourself from that place where you feel - against all logic - that it must have something to do with you and therefore you continue to feel not as optimal as you could until this element that is external to the relationship has been resolved.

An example that is slightly closer to home is when the partner actually feels upset or annoyed or impatient or jealous or whatever about something *you* have done - or he/she simply believes you have done, and you are now in this not-so-good-place with regards to how he/she behaves with you. Thus your inner world tends to collapse, and you will often do whatever it takes to re-establish the equilibrium.

That's what it means being glued together at the hip. And it's not a pretty picture. Not for you and not for your partner because he/she will have similar reactions, even though one of the two may notice it more than the other, or hide it better than the other. That is generally the *dominant partner*.

Here's the thing: until you are emotionally *independent* of your partner in the sense that you are taking such good care of yourself on all levels including the one where you love yourself, and unless you have reached a point where your responsibility for yourself embraces absolutely all aspects of your life, you will not be able to totally unglue yourself from the hip of the other. This is a process that begins with becoming aware of exactly what is going on.

So this quest to find autonomy in love begins in some ways by freeing yourself from some of the bonds. Let's imagine that your partner has indicated that for some reason he/she is upset with you. Or, God forbid, that they may be contemplating abandoning you. You are devastated. Even in the milder case, where it's merely a question of an upset between the two of you. *You recognize this feeling. You have been here many times before.* What it is telling you is that *your well-being depends on your partner being OK with you.* It depends on him/her not being angry or annoyed with you. This sense of well-being that sways back and forth depending on how your partner is feeling about you *enslaves you.* Not your partner. Your partner is not the one who is enslaving you, although at times it may feel like that. It is your own inner well-being or lack of it wavering back and forth according to your partner's moods that enslaves you. And let's reiterate: this is most definitely *not* about it being your partner's responsibility to ensure *your* well-being by behaving differently. It's about you taking on that responsibility for *yourself.*

So this is what is necessary: your own recognition that when you feel like that, *it is up to you to change how you feel, no matter what is going on with your partner at all.* The reason you waver in that fashion is because your own inner core, your inner emotional core is not strong. *It needs the approbation or love of the other to allow it to feel good.* If you can begin to understand this, you will see that the wavering comes from you and not from outside of you. It comes from a lack of love for yourself. What will make it strong, bit by bit, is if you begin to show the self that you love the self *enough to take care of the self* in moments like the one described, *by being good to the self and doing something that will make you feel better at that moment in time, despite your partner's mood.*

This process will strengthen something that is not very strong in you: the love you have for yourself, and if you do this at any time you feel that familiar negative sensation referred to above, then each time you *choose to care for the self and choose to re-establish that inner balance and well-being despite the outer circumstance*, you will grow in self love. And that will bring you to freedom from the bonds.

Truth

And of course this brings us to the endlessly and infinitely essential topic of the fact that truth must come before all else. In relationships of any kind *truth must indeed come before all else.* And that truth is the backbone and *prana* - life breath and life blood - of any relationship, call it friendship, marriage, or inter-family relationship.

Without truth, or transparency, if you will, and an emphasis in your relationships on the vital importance of truth, *very little flourishes*, at least over time.

Truth is essential for trust, truth is essential for growth (although growth can also take place in the absence of truth when people recognize its absence and take measures of one kind or another), and truth is essential for joy. Relationships without a good measure of trust, growth, and joy may be a lot less than what you really want present in your life.

And remember, truth is not limited to not lying. Another kind of lying that may ultimately poison the relationship may appear for example, when people refuse to acknowledge any problems, acting as though *nothing is wrong.*

Basically what this boils down to, is that when talking about truth it's also important to take into consideration its *lack by omission*, as well as when one is pretending things are different from what they are – both to oneself, and to the other person (or people) involved in the relationship.

You might liken truth to the first bud that appears in the spring and the last red leaf that falls from the tree in the late fall. Truth must be present at the beginning and at the end. Truth towards oneself, and truth towards others.

If truth is not present, little else can thrive. With truth, transformation, growth, and ultimately inner freedom have a chance. Truth. Think of it as your greatest challenge and your greatest friend.

Expressing All Your Emotions

A further aspect of vast significance in the process of growth - and very connected to the issue of not lying and telling the truth - is recognizing the need for and learning how to express all your emotions. On occasion it may sound as though I am suggesting that you focus only on feeling good, on keeping your energetic vibration or frequency high, and that you ignore or forget about your other, less agreeable emotions.

In fact, nothing could be further from the truth.

Your emotions need careful looking at, careful calibration, and certainly, should not be ignored. If you are angry, this needs to be expressed. If you are sad, or grieving, again, this needs to be expressed. If you are feeling any kind of emotion, an avenue for its expression needs to be found. But the expression of your emotion needs to be a healthy one.

So if you are angry, yelling, fighting, or insulting won't cut it. A healthy expression might be something along the lines of maintaining healthy boundaries as discussed in various sections of this book, where you could choose to say to the person who has angered you: that is not acceptable to me. Or: your lack of respect (or consideration) for me is inacceptable. Or: I feel that you have not listened to me, not understood me, and I feel that you are totally ignoring my opinions about this matter. This makes me feel insulted (or hurt, or angry, or sad, etc.).

The salient point is that as you express your emotions in this way, rather than by fighting, or arguing, or playing the one-upmanship game, you are showing yourself respect for yourself, and thus gain a sense of empowerment.

If the emotions you are feeling are grief or sadness, these must also be expressed. If someone you love is ill, or if you have lost someone you love, or if you have had a loss of another kind, you clearly cannot gloss over this, and try to make yourself feel good. You must go through the process of the loss, or the pain. Nevertheless, the healthy personality will find – even in a situation of this nature – first, a way to return to inner balance, and second, something positive to take from it, something to learn from it, something with which inner growth can take place, leading to ever greater inner freedom. Most particularly, as we have seen, such a person will be sufficiently aware, self-responsible, and self-loving to establish a measure of inner balance before going on.

Here is where renowned thinkers or world leaders such as Viktor Frankl (*Man's Search For Meaning*), or Nelson Mandela (his autobiography), or Alexandr Solzhenitsyn's autobiographical work *One Day in the Life of Ivan Denisovich,* can help open your eyes a great deal due to their own examples of inner fortitude and the decisions they made on a daily basis - no matter what their external circumstances - in order to maintain that inner balance.

Doing this consciously on a daily basis leads to growth of a kind that will also further you on the path to spiritual partnership. Indeed, my deepest desire for you is your growth, understanding, and transformation. Inner freedom is a choice you are free to make. As long as you take on the quest for continual awareness in the myriad ways discussed here in this book, you *will* begin the refashioning of your inner world and with it, your outer world will also be transformed.

Conclusion:

The Promise of Conscious Spiritual Partnerships

The multiple relationship scenarios described throughout this book all begin with two individuals who are not aware of themselves. By not having awareness, they are also - obviously - not aware of their partner in any true sense. This is not a question of intelligence, education, or demographics. When the ego is in play, when what they feel inside is pain or frustration or anger, and they believe that it rests on the shoulder of the partner, what causes them to begin to look inward rather than outward is much less a case of who their parents are, where they lived, and how brilliantly or not they finished their academic education, and then went on to an important professional position, but a case of how much they desire to not continue living in this tortured way. But before they reach that point, they react blindly, they blame, they insist that the partner has changed and is no longer the loving, charming, or ideal person he or she was when they first fell in love.

They are totally unaware of the fact that the patterns in their own life have brought them to such an impasse (as have the patterns of the partner brought him or her to that same place), as they are also totally unaware of the fact that by the resolution of precisely what they are complaining or unhappy about, they could find their way towards a conscious spiritual partnership. But resolving does not mean 'fixing' the partner so that he is once again the person he appeared to be when they fell in love. Resolving hinges on their own decision to walk down a road towards self-awareness where they realize that each and every pebble, stone or boulder they stumble over, is an opportunity to come closer to themselves and to the partner because of what the impediment can show them about their own inner nature.

Hence the need to not only become aware, but also to love the self, to take on total responsibility for one's own well-being, and in general, realize that just as examinations at school were a way of proceeding on to the next level, so too, does relationship frustration and pain offer a brilliantly unique opportunity for growth and self-understanding.

Transcending the current situation and moving to a spiritual partnership is not so much a question of rational understanding as a matter of implementation by conscious practice, fueled by intention and attention. It begs the question: do you want to do this? Do you want such a partnership, as opposed to the kind of relationship you have had all your life? Because of course it will only ever materialize in your life if you do want it, and hence begin to take some of the suggested steps.

Having embarked on this venture, in parallel fashion another valuable transformation begins to take place - by intending to remain conscious and applying such awareness to the issues that arise in the relationship, each of the partners almost automatically not only seeks greater connection to the self, but also to the other. Such connection is paramount to the growth into spiritual partnership and likewise into loving and understanding the self. These are enormous steps in personal evolution when they are in fact undertaken.

The two individuals involved in the evolving partnership begin to grasp the key role inner connection plays, not only in their daily interaction, but in the ways in which the partnership begins to shift and develop into something that bears little resemblance to their former conventional relationship. The way in which the two interact, the way they relate to each other foments not only a more profound love on levels that go beyond the love experienced during the conventional phase of the relationship, precisely because of the burgeoning inner connection between the two, but this new interaction also foments another kind of sexuality. When a soul touches a soul something different sparks between two partners, than when mere chemistry - no matter how exciting - is all that is in play. In order for souls to connect, the inner connection in each of the two with themselves must have already been established, or at least must be an ongoing individual process.

A spiritual partnership is spiritual not only because the partners view the partnership as a growth-enhancing path, or *tao*, but also because the partners have come to recognize that their connection to each other is not only from this lifetime. Let me hasten to clarify that I'm not talking about soul mates. The two individuals I'm talking about may be that - or not. But what I do believe, is that they have been connected before now and they are together precisely in order to learn whatever they can through this partnership so that they no longer need to repeat these lessons. In this sense, the evolution that takes place, or that *can* take place, is that the partners are now on an entirely different soul level where they can transcend from where they have been up to this point and begin the exhilarating process of moving to new growth and evolution.

They may have spent lifetimes being a victim, a perpetrator, a blamer, a close-minded and judgmental criticizer, an intolerant and cold autocrat, a needy, submissive, and bleeding heart, or anything at all, but now, thanks to the growth that is taking place in this spiritual partnership, they are able to leave that behind, because this is one lesson they no longer need to learn. If your soul has ever formed part of your agenda, or if you have begun to recognize (and joined the legions who have also recognized this) that you do indeed, have a soul and that you are so much more than just your physical self, then this is a path you can follow in order to re-create the eternal connection you may have forgotten about.

This is the promise of spiritual partnership. Evolution and growth become concrete realities, both personally as well as within the relationship, but not only on those more mundane (albeit very significant) levels of our psyche and emotions, but also - and most especially - on the level of our spirit: our soul. Spiritual partnership offers the potential to be one of the most brilliant ways to move into a life of soul and a life with soul.

APPENDIX

Beauty, Gratitude & Mindfulness Exercise

Choose a time, during daylight hours when you can walk unimpeded, on your own, for 15 minutes. Start by focusing on the beauty around you, whether this is beauty you see, smell, hear, taste or touch. It can be a flower, plant, or tree, the perfume of a rose, birdsong, clouds, blue sky, fresh-smelling rain, the beautifully executed corner of an architecturally pleasing building, a blade of grass, or green shoots emerging from charred wood. When you do this, also allow yourself to feel gratitude for whatever it is you are perceiving with one or more of your senses. This brings you into the present moment, allowing your mind to be still. Notice the sensation - albeit brief - of momentary peace. Then do it again, by noticing something else you consider beautiful, and again, feel the gratitude and again notice the inner peace. Try to continue doing this for the entire 15 minutes. If at one point you realize your thoughts have wandered off to your worries or past pain, or just everyday problems, don't get annoyed with yourself. Simply pull yourself back to noticing beauty again until your 15 minutes are up. The more often you do this, the longer you will be able to remain focused on beauty, and the more your neural pathways will change. These are neural pathways that allow you to experience a feeling of well-being not only when you are doing the exercise, but also during the rest of your day, especially after having practiced the exercise for some time.

Forgiveness Exercise

- Think of a painful event from your past
- Now say to yourself: I know what it was that happened in my past that somehow pushes painful buttons in my present and causes me to go into this place where I hurt so much.
- Do I want to be here? Or do I prefer to find a way out of this morass?

- Here the typical answer is: *yes, I want to be out of here, but it's impossible because this is what always happens now because of what happened then, in my past. I can't do anything about it. I've tried and it doesn't work.*

- So now you tell yourself: "Well, I may not be able to resolve this right now, but I am able to *choose to focus on something else.* Focusing on something else doesn't mean that I'm pretending this is no longer important, but it *does* mean that by focusing elsewhere I am giving myself the opportunity to come to a better place inside of me, a higher energetic frequency, so that from that better place, I can review the situation."

- I may focus on something I am grateful for in my life, or something I am grateful for in the place in which I currently find myself, in order to bring myself to the *now*, to the present moment, because if I am in the present moment, and furthermore in a space of gratitude, I will automatically feel better even if only for a few minutes. In that moment, in the now, there is no room for thoughts of future worries or past pain.

- I may go for a brisk 20-30 minute walk and during the walk only focus on the sensations in my body as I walk, as well as being grateful for whatever I feel and observe around me, in order to remain in the present by being mindful.

- Now that I feel better – even if only slightly – I will ask myself if I want to forgive whomever or whatever happened when I was younger that keeps creating present pain.

- My answer may be that what happened to me cannot be forgiven. My answer may be that I want to forgive, but that I can't. I may have tried in the past and found it to be impossible. Or my answer may be that I want to forgive but don't know how.

- In all these examples, the salient point is that *if you do not forgive, whether you believe what happened is unforgivable, or whether you believe that you cannot or do not know how to forgive, the energetic connection to the past will not be broken, and you will continue to feel the pain.* If, however, you decide to take on the process of forgiving *for your own sake and for your own healing, and above all, because you love yourself so much* (or would *like* to love yourself so much) *that you want this to be gone from your life,* then you will do it.

- Here's how, in a nutshell: each time something happens to bring the pain into the present, or each time you remember the event from the past, and hence re-visit the initial pain, tell yourself that your intention is to forgive. *My intention is to forgive. I may not know how, but I intend to forgive. And because I intend to forgive, right now, instead of continuing to focus on the pain (or the anger, or whatever the negative feeling is), I will focus on something life-giving, something I can feel gratitude for, something that keeps me here in the present moment.*
- Each time you do this with awareness and conscious choice, you are strengthening a new neural pathway and weakening an old one. Each time you do this with awareness and conscious choice, you are affirming your love for yourself. And the more you do it with awareness and conscious choice, the more you will have forgiven – for your sake, and for your health and well-being and thus will have furthered the love for yourself.

Self-Talk Exercise

Just as an experiment, I'd like you to try an exercise for the next week. Make a list of about ten qualities or aspects or characteristics about your partner that you really enjoy and appreciate (even if lately they seem to have gotten lost in the shuffle). Look at that list on a daily basis. Think about the items on the list, remember some of the times in the past – before your current bickering - when they were in evidence on a regular basis. Whenever you find yourself thinking about the unpleasant aspects of your partner, or what he or she said or did (or didn't say or do) last week, the other day, or this morning, *deliberately* change your thoughts towards your list, and think about the good things about your partner, rather than about the negative ones. Focus on the good traits. Refuse to think about the negative ones. Just for one week.

I would love to hear some of the results of this little experiment, but my guess, judging by the results achieved by my clients, is that a good number of those who try it will be surprised to realize that things went better than usual. They may even say that it was just one of those weeks that was less difficult than others. Hmm. Could it be possible that it had something to do with the thoughts that were being focused on; the positive aspects of the partner rather than the negative? Could it be possible that the more you think about something ... *anything* ... the more precisely that will appear in your life? This is, after all, what all the afore-mentioned thinkers and researchers have said. Focus on the negative aspects of your partner, and your life will be filled with them. Focus on the positive ones and note the difference in what happens.

I invite you to try similar experiments about whatever it is that plagues you. Do I hear someone saying that this is impossible? A pipe dream, because thoughts creep unbidden into the mind and one can't control them? Did I say this is easy? How did you learn how to use your computer? How did you grow nearly non-existent bicep muscles into a hard, firm, well-toned upper arm? How did you learn that foreign language? How did you learn how to play tennis? Was it not with some practice and discipline? Of course. And so it is with this. Realize that in order to grapple with your thoughts; in order to find some measure of control over them in such a way that they *speak the language* that most approximates whatever it is that you wish to see or realize in your life, you must practice *changing* the thoughts that do not lead you in that direction into another kind of thoughts.

And this is only possible with practice. Just because we are talking about your thoughts and not muscles or the grammatical structure of a new language, does not mean that discipline isn't an important aspect of it. For a time, particularly at the beginning of your journey down this wonderful pathway, you will need to spend a good portion of your leisure time practicing this endeavor. Reminding yourself of it. Recognizing over and over again, that once again you forgot, and then, just like a child who is learning how to walk, and falls, and gets up, and falls again, and gets up again, and again, and again, and again, you also, will get up as often as is necessary, in order to come to a point, where this new way of thinking becomes a well-ingrained habit. And of course, as indicated in the chapters on thoughts and emotions, use your feelings to get a handle on your thoughts. It is much easier to pay conscious attention to your inner state of being, than to your thoughts. But – your feelings will inform you very explicitly about what's going on with your thoughts. And that's the place where – from a position of awareness – choice, self-love and self-responsibility can come into play in order to change the tenor of those thoughts.

Maintaining Your Inner State of Energy High

This is not so much an exercise, as the intelligent use of sources that offer video, audio or simply text files that may change your energy. You will have to find the ones that actually resonate with you, and the selection provided here is taken from my blog.

These are links that offer much valuable material; some of them carry a cost, but most do not. Have a look for yourself to see which ones help *you* change your inner energetic frequency.

What I suggest, is that you download some of the material offered, load them into your phone or i-Pod, or burn them to CD's, or whatever you use, and then listen to them *at least* 15-20 minutes per day. An easy way to do this is to have access to a collection of them in your car, and to listen to them while you drive to and from work. Another suggestion would be to listen while you are shaving, putting on your make-up, or cooking (assuming you are alone in the kitchen). *Notice* how your energy shifts as you listen or watch. It's similar to having a vitamin pill for your spirit.

Using such tools will quickly make a definitive difference in your energetic frequency, and more importantly, in how you view your world, how you react, and how aware you remain.

By typing the following url into your computer, you will have immediate access the pdf file containing the most current list of links: http://tinyurl.com/8ru5jxs

or use the QR Code embedded on the next page:

Bibliography

In *Rewiring the Soul* I included about 40 pages of Bibliography prefaced with the following words:

Why does a book as deceptively simple as this one require such an extensive bibliography? It doesn't. Nevertheless, these books are a portion of those that have shaped my life and in so doing have shaped my thoughts and my understanding. And it is in the shaping of these that this book could be written so simply and so directly. Psychology, neuroscience, biology, sociology, history, politics, religion, spirituality, philosophy, mythology, dreams and fairy tales, body work, metaphysics and esoteric thought, motivational books, biographies and autobiographies all form part of this mélange, as well as some journals of certain writers or thinkers and several dozen novels that have also been included because they too, were significant.

I have returned over and over again to some of these books, as one returns to old and loved friends; friends that are beloved because of what has been shared and because of the support that has been given, and what has been learned. Sometimes, however, I return to a book, no longer certain if I remember it, and then I see the highlighting, the underlining and the scribbled notes on *precisely* those passages that still resonate with me now, and that reminded me then, when I first read them, of what I really already knew. *Just as you do.* It's not really important if you look at this list at all. But perhaps you'll enjoy doing so.

The Tao of Spiritual Partnership is built on those books as well, because as I say above, these books shaped me and my thinking. But I hope you understand that in order to keep the publishing cost of this book down, those many pages will not be included again.

However, you can access them all here online by going to this link: http://tinyurl.com/9uz4sza which will automatically open a pdf file of the Bibliography, or by using the QR Code embedded on the next page:

Index